35 PRINCIPLES FOR
LASTING LIFE CHANGE

35 PRINCIPLES FOR LASTING LIFE CHANGE

The guide of practical solutions to everyday problems

JACOB AKLEY & MICHAEL BENSON

Akley & Benson Consulting 2022

DEDICATIONS

For my three boys, Jaiden, Urijah, and Miles,
I hope as you grow and learn to understand these principles, you become the men you know you are capable of. My passion is to help mold and nurture your talents, and minds. You three taught me selflessness instead of selfishness, to give rather than take, and to love unconditionally. Give your gifts to the world, and you will always find fulfillment.
Chase your "Something" I love you boys,
I would also like to thank my co-author, my best friend, my brother for his invaluable insights and tireless revisions throughout this process. This book wouldn't have happened with out you my friend.

DEDICATIONS

Zeus, Carlee, Gio and Sophia, you are all endowed with extraordinary gifts! I believe in you and your capacity to learn, grow and become the role models you were born to be. You have shown me the power of influence and the value of refined leadership. You've inspired me to live each day with excitement and vigorous enthusiasm. You are the reason I wake up every morning, hungry, ready to attack the day. You've ignited a fire inside that is fueled with unconditional love. I would also like to acknowledge and give thanks to my mother, and best friend Jacob. Mom, you patiently looked after and cared for my children while I took the time to write this book. I appreciate all that you've done and will always be indebted to you. Jacob, you've inspired me to live at my highest potential and to achieve all that I can become. I appreciate your friendship and look forward to a life long pursuit of becoming our best selves.

FOREWORD

Thank you for picking this book up, it means you want to see change in your life. Often times we have dreams, and goals that get buried from our everyday life, and distractions. These ultimately lead to poor attitudes, sadness, anger, resentment, decline in our behavior, and a lack of belief in ourselves. What about the feeling of being lost, or being unable to climb out of our own self-pity? I know because I've been there. My mom died when I was 8 years old, I never knew my biological father, I was poor, abused, and on government assistance. I dropped out of high school, went to jail, was homeless with a new born, suffering from emotional distress. I had a choice, I could throw a pity party, and I did for years. Or I could change my ways. I found that nothing was going to change until I did. I picked up a few disciplines, and got obsessed with self-development. I realized that if I kept doing what I was doing, I was going to keep getting what I had. After reading more than 400 books by the most significant minds in self-help and personal development, I, with the help of my coauthor and dear friend Mike, saw that there were 35 principles that stood the test of time. Principles that transcended across every book we read. These principles hold true no matter who you are, your color, gender, creed, or even where you come from. As you read you may find many of these principles are intertwined and woven into one another, as it takes all for one to succeed. Practice these, and implement them. This book is designed to read one principal a week! Yes you read that right. It is simple but, it is absolutely necessary you follow the guidelines of the exercises laid out in the pages that follow, as this is designed to offer you practical everyday use of these 35 principles. Studies show reading something multiple times, versus once, have significant impacts on increased retention and implementation. So every day for one week, you will focus & implement one principle. Each principal is a maximum of 2 pages. This is intentional. If it's easy and simple to do, more will be willing to try. The two pages contain one principle, problems caused by the lack of the principle, and solutions to implement the principle into your daily routine. Practice every day builds habits, and habits become personality traits. You will see changes in your life in every area, and aspect, if you choose to! I went through all I went through to now owning multiple businesses, traveling the world, living life on my terms, and empowering others to see & live their dreams. I can teach you what stands the test of time, but it's up to you to apply what you read, and learn. I hope you find everyday practical use out of this book, and that it helps you manifest the life you want to live. I know you can do it because I did it. Remember, life's a marathon not a sprint. Keep chasing, I'll see you at the finish line.

-Jacob Akley

FOREWORD

Four years ago, an old fishing dock illuminated by the moon's grace carried two young men discussing their place in life. With 30 years of existence and not much to show for it, they understood that for their lives to change, they had to change themselves. -And so began the endless pursuit of self-mastery... Realizing the priceless impact made in our lives, Jacob and I decided to pay it forward and take the time to outline our most cataclysmic findings. We employ these principles on a continual basis and practice the tactics laid out in this book to offer living proof of their transformative capabilities. Even though I've come a long way in my journey I understand that still, I have an eternity to go, and the choices I make will determine my future. We're always faced with choices in life which stack up revealing our character or lack thereof. I wish that when my time here is complete, I will have led by positive example and unwavering integrity. Personal development is an infinite process and continues to remind us of the fact several times throughout life. The moment we start to think we've got it all figured out we're smacked in the face and taken for a wild ride without warning. Arrogance gets us nowhere and ignorance is not bliss. They say what we don't know won't hurt us, but that's false. Suppose you were driving and didn't know the red traffic light meant stop. It's not likely to produce a blissful experience for us. And assuming just makes, well you know, ass-u-me. We need accurate information and the more practical it's use, the better. This book was designed to be practical and informative, and easy to digest. Allow it to be your guide through the storms of life and practice each principle as if the quality of your life depends on it, because it does. I hope you follow the instructions given as they will help you make use of each principle and commit them to memory. I believe you are capable of doing great things! The question is: "Will you?"

-Michael Benson

TABLE OF CONTENTS

PRINCIPLE 1 HABITS

"We are what we repeatedly do. Excellence, then, is not
an act but a habit."

–Aristotle

A habit is a settled or regular tendency or practice,
especially one that is hard to give up.

Problem:

When you're feeling bruised and broken, your brain goes
into habit mode. You find in continuing to repeat this day in
and day out, that you have fallen out of some good habits
you used to practice. Review what your habits are, in doing
so you will find some of them just might be hindering your
forward progress. Maybe you used to stay at your particular
sports practice longer than you do now, or how you used to
read the books, but now you find you're not. You used to
show up to work early but now you show up late. That's why
it is so important for us to cultivate good habits. Get back
into those habits, it's a part of discipline and commitment.

Success takes a certain set of skills practiced everyday as
habits. It's the habit to get up early every day, the habit of
hard work, to commit time to studying and developing. It's
in giving more, and becoming more. If it were easy everyone
would do it. How you spend your 24 hours determines who
you become. Remember the billionaire and the beggar both
have 24 hours, the secret to their success or failure is in their

daily routines. So let's talk about how to get out of bad habits and into good habits.

Solutions:

How do you start your day

Most people wake up every morning and begin thinking about yesterday's problems, and in doing so repeat the same behavior and subsequently the same habits. So then the solution would be to start our day thinking about what we are grateful for rather than a matter or situation that's unwelcome or harmful. One way to do that is to get a sheet of paper and write 1-10, then list 10 things you are currently grateful for in your life. You'll find in doing this, a natural state of euphoria and creativity emerge. Cultivating the habit of stacking gratitude can significantly increase your productivity throughout the day. This week take time to build the habit of stacking gratitude each morning when you arise. In doing this you will start to cultivate good habits again.

Analyzing your 24 hours

The best way for you to examine how your day has been spent is to write it down. The same is true for your week, month, and year. In tracking how you spend your time each day, you can then hold yourself to a higher standard by knowing what you're achieving and what you're not. There is a certain type of magic that arises when you identify a problem, because only when a problem is identified can we find a solution. For the next week, write down how you are spending your 24 hours. After assessing, you can clearly see what habits are serving you and which ones are not. Then start changing the habit patterns that do not serve you, and focus more on the ones that do. It's imperative you follow these steps. For change to happen, you have to change.

Sacrifice who you are for who you can be

You see in giving up the habits we hold now, and in cultivating new and empowering habits, we start to change our personal identity. We should always want to change and become the best versions of ourselves. Who you were doesn't have to be who you become. Take time this week to decide who you want to be, and then start living like you are already that person. What you will find in acting like the individual you want to become, is that you practice the habits that individual would have. We are what we repeatedly do. What are you doing?

PRINCIPLE 2 PRACTICE

"Practice doesn't make perfect. Practice makes perme-
ances."

-Eric Thomas

Practice can be described as the customary, habitual, or
expected procedure or way of doing of something.

Problem:

We've heard practice makes perfect. We teach practice
leads to habitual behavior. That is to say that anything we do
over and over becomes a habit and rewires our mind and
body to do it better the next time. We become what we
repeatedly do. Our practices form our habits which dictate
our lifestyles. All too often we fail to realize that we're
ALWAYS practicing something; the question is what?
Unfortunately, most people are usually distracting themselves with something like television or the radio, or whatever they can find on their cellphone. They prioritize the
things they want to do, over the things they should really be
focused on. It doesn't take long at all before they start forgetting to do this or forgetting to do that because it wasn't a
priority. Even if unconsciously practicing distraction, we
seamlessly form the inability to focus and begin to take on
the attribute we call distracted. When we see this in our
children, we seek medical advice but often they're mis-
diagnosed and labeled with attention deficit hyperactivity

disorder (ADHD). Consider what you've been practicing, both wittingly and unwittingly, and asses where you can implement more intentional practices. Below are a few ideas to help you see the importance of practice and how to perform it more deliberately.

Solutions:

Direction

When we know what we want in our lives we can gather a good sense of direction and with that, understand what we should be focused on practicing. The young NBA all-star knows what we wants and where he's projecting his life to be. In order to manifest that goal into his reality, he understands he'll need to practice all the fundamentals of basketball, and the importance of doing it daily. He doesn't mind showing up early, bringing his best attitude and staying late because he can see where this commitment to himself will eventually get him. He is intentional with his time and deliberately engages in the necessary practices that will move him in the direction of his vision. Take time this week to write out and describe what direction you are currently headed and where you would like to be. This is your map! Utilize it and determine what practices are aiding you and which are not on your journey to your ideal future. Commit to the ones that are serving your purpose and eliminate everything else.

Skills

Have you ever wanted to become proficient at something? Of course, you have! When you were a baby you were eager to walk because while you lie helplessly on the floor, you see mom or dad up on their feet, getting anywhere they'd like to be. Perhaps you saw big brother or big sister getting into the cookie jar and you knew that you just had to find out what that tasty treat was. Whatever the reason, you were determined to stand up and try, and try until you had gotten it right. You fell down but it didn't discourage you, instead you found your way back your feet and with just as much enthusiasm as before. You were still young but understood that if you kept trying, then you would eventually walk. You didn't realize it then but you were building resiliency, laying the very foundation needed for acquiring every other skillset throughout life, resiliency. Take time this week to write out what skills you've developed so far and how you've come to obtain them. Take inventory of yourself. Everybody wants to be valuable and one of the best ways we can achieve that is to continuously develop and improve our skills. Think about where you're going in life and what skills you'll need to develop in order to get there. Remember, we form our skills through deliberate and consistent practice, and it all comes down to your level of commitment to the process.

Repetition

We've all heard that repetition is the mother of skill. Every time you repeat a process, you become more familiar with it and find yourself not having to think about it as much. We call this muscle memory. This process creates maximum efficiency within the motor and memory systems allowing us to operate more fluently. Think back to a time you really wanted to get good at something. Anything. A dance maybe? If you remember correctly, you weren't the best at it the first time you tried. However, you knew that you might get it right if you tried again, so you gave it a go. You didn't mind making a fool of yourself, in fact, you enjoyed it. You were having fun and didn't mind putting in the necessary reps because you were learning something that really interested you. Repetition helps us build strength, both physically and mentally. The fact is simple; we can strengthen any area of our lives that we desire if we are willing to put in the reps. Take time this week to write down what you don't mind deliberately practicing and what you're a bit apprehensive towards. This list will help highlight your gifts. Strengthen them. Remember, if you want something badly enough, the price will be easy to pay.

Principle 3 Character

"Character cannot be developed in ease and quiet. Only through experience of trial and suffering can the soul be strengthened, ambition inspired, and success achieved."

-Helen Keller

Character is defined as the mental and moral qualities distinctive to an individual.

Problem:

Having a lack of character can produce social imbalances causing you to disrespect others. When you lack character you lack in other areas as well, particularly in self-esteem and self-worth. You character or lack thereof typically shows in how you treat others. Having a lack of character means your integrity is compromised. When we falter in character every other area of our lives suffer. How can we mold ourselves to be people of character? Let's find out below.

Solutions:

Know Thy Self

In knowing who you are and what you stand for, you chisel the master piece of your life.

Character comes from the Greek word that means chisel or the mark left by a chisel. As we chisel away habits that are continuously stopping us from achieving more we start to shape our character, one choice at a time, moment by moment. We are either chipping away the bad stuff and creating our character, or we are chipping away the good and soon the marble will crumble. The person who doesn't stand for anything will fall for everything. What are you doing when nobody is watching? Those moments are what truly shape our character and make us who we are. This week take time to ask yourself what your values are, and what do you stand for? Ask yourself if opposition were to come, would you stand or fall for what you believe in. History revels in the individuals who were willing to risk their life for the values they hold to be true. They knew who they were and they knew what they believed in. Do you know who you are? Are you proud of the character you've built?

Compassion

Having concern for the sufferings or misfortunes of others can fulfill us in ways we have never imagined. When you have to ability to comfort an individual in pain, or giving a life vest to a person going through a storm, people feel a sense of belief that they can count on you to help them when they need it. We have all been in places in life where we needed someone to come rescue us from oblivion. Maybe our spouse left us, or a family member died. We need direction, and guidance. We need someone to show us the light when we are in the darkness. Compassion literally means "to suffer together." You are willing to help someone else because you can feel how they feel, in turn you feel motivated to help relive their suffering. Compassion largely impacts our character. Take time this week to have compassion for someone suffering and help them if you can. The feeling we get in helping others is truly a gift you can only experience in the doing.

Humility

The beginning of wisdom is in humility. For us to build our character we have to be open to new ways and viewpoints. When we become selfless, we lose selfishness. Humility is most certainly an essential piece of the character we manifest through acknowledging others, being empathetic, and respecting them at a deeper level, while at the same time we understand and own our own limitations. Psychologists have established links between humility and how we learn to be effective leaders. Take time this week to learn more about humility and how you can apply it in areas of your life. In doing this you will really start to chisel your character in ways you never imagined.

Principle 4 Charity

"The smallest act of kindness is worth more than the grandest intention."

-Oscar Wilde

Charity is defined as the voluntary giving of help to those in need.

Problem:

Have you ever been so hungry your stomach feels like it's eating itself? Maybe you ate good growing up, but your parents didn't have the money to get you new clothes or shoes. How did it feel? You wanted to have a full belly and the new shoes, but the pain of seeing someone you know wearing what you didn't have made you feel insignificant. There are an estimated 580,466 people in the United States experiencing homelessness on a given night, according to the most recent national point-in-time estimate (January 2020). This represents a rate of approximately 18 people experiencing homelessness per every 10,000 people in the general population. An increase of roughly 3.6% since 2019. Over half a million adults, kids, and even infants are going without food or shelter tonight. They will sleep on cardboard under a bridge, or perhaps by a tree in a park. Urine and fecal matter cover the streets, with drug abuse, mental illness and neglect. I know because I have seen it firsthand. I was in California one weekend on business. Driving through the Hollywood hills, fine dining in Beverly Hills, and Malibu, but there is a side of these glamorous cities that most don't see. Just on the outskirts are homeless encampments as far as the eye can see.

The biggest section is called "Skid Row" in Los Angeles. If you haven't seen what true poverty looks like, take a drive down this 52 block encampment. The smells alone can give a man perspective. There is hope, and it starts with a question.

How can we help those who can't help themselves?

Solutions:

Giving

Giving starts the receiving process. T.D. Jakes said, "..Unless you learn to give for what you get it will die. Reciprocity. What do you give for what you get?" There is a certain type of fulfillment that is cultivated through the process of giving that is not obtainable in any other way. Also the person receiving has an overwhelming sense of gratitude toward you. They may even shed a tear. Human beings are meant to give and help each other. We are all one people, each projecting their individualism through these vehicles we call bodies. So then in the process of giving, we get. We get both physical and mental stimulation through helping someone in need. Think about a time you did something good for another person. How did you feel in that moment? Say your neighbor dropped their wallet. You could leave it, take it, or return it. You did the right thing and gave it back to them. In the process you and the owner in that exact moment are sharing a surge in serotonin or what we call the (gratitude chemical). The owner is extremely grateful you returned their property, and you are happy to see them happy. That is what giving is all about. Take time this week to notice when you have an opportunity to practice giving. The important thing is, if you could give, and should give, and you don't, you're on the wrong track. Take the opportunity to give each day this week, and watch how it comes back into your life. It could be a smile, or a helping hand. Remember we reap what we sow.

Teaching

"If you give a man a fish, you'll feed him for a day. If you teach a man to fish, you'll feed him for a life time." What happens when we teach someone a new life skill? In teaching a new skill, we have opened their minds to new possibilities. We can teach the hopeless to hope again, teach the broke how to obtain wealth, we can teach the fallen how to stand back up, and we can teach people how to belief in life again. Those are all possibilities on the chess board of life, and it's up to us to decide what moves we make. We can teach abundance, how to think, prosperity, health, and wealth, or we can perpetuate poverty, mediocrity and generality. Teaching also teaches the teacher. We are tested in how we approach every situation, and each one is different. We are building the plane as we go. We are learning every day. Techers are lifelong learners. The price is easy when the promise is strong. You have a choice on what you teach your brother, your sister, your mom, or your kids. What are you giving through teaching; Abundance or despair? Take time this week to analyze what you are teaching the people around you. Are you teaching them how to be, and do more? Create a plan of action this week to teach something positive to at least 5 people. It's not in what we get, but who we become in the process.

Random acts of kindness

These can be some of the simplest tasks. Maybe you're holding the door open for an elderly person, or helping someone pick up a pile of papers they dropped. Maybe you were in traffic and someone in the car next to you is screaming at the stop light and you simply smile and break their state. Random acts of kindness could be telling a stranger they are beautiful inside and out, man or woman, not for any other purpose but to remind them they are someone. Those simple everyday experiences can literally change a person's state from upset to smiling, from angry to happy. The great part about random acts of kindness is when other people see you doing that, they feel the urge to want to do the same. Random acts of kindness could change someone's day. When you realize you have the power to alter someone's day and emotional state, why wouldn't you do it? Jim Rohn said, "Be better not bitter. " Take time each day this week to practice a random act of kindness. Whether it's a hand or a smile, give it away.

Principle 5 Discipline

"Discipline is the bridge between goals and accomplishment."

–Jim Rohn

Discipline is a set of rules or behaviors practiced on consistent basis to achieve a set goal or desired outcome.

Problem:

How does discipline affect what you do and who you are as an individual? Let's imagine you want to lose weight. This is an almost universal desire in western culture. Maybe you jog around the block, take a walk, go to the gym, or pick up a new and healthy activity, but in the process you continue to feed your body with pizza and pop instead of salad and water? What will be the underlying result of your lack of discipline in this particular area? Obviously, you aren't going to become healthier, because you've neglected the daily discipline to eat the right foods day in and day out. As a result, the outcome you are seeking will be unattainable and fleeting. Which leads to lack of motivation and inspiration.

So then, how do we cultivate the skill set of discipline? Meaning, how do we do what we said we were going to do, long after the mood we have said it in has left?

Solutions:

Here are a few simple practices that if implemented into

your daily routine will help you become a master of self-discipline in your life.

Resolve

Resolve means you've made a decision and it doesn't matter if it's easy or hard, you're going to do it. Let's say you're adamant about being on a sports team at your high school. To obtain a spot on the team you have to have many small forms of discipline. It's the discipline to get good grades and study in class. It's the discipline to practice day in and day out. The discipline to show up early and stay late. It's the discipline to keep going even when you want to stop. If you're willing to live your life like others won't, then you'll have the life that others want. It's not just the sports team these practices extended across. You could want to be an artists, singer, writer, or actor. None the less they apply to all.

Commitment

Commitment means you are dedicated to a cause or activity no matter the circumstance. It means you are willing to make the necessary sacrifices to see your dreams actualized, to not only say but do what you intend. This is a principle that needs further discussion that we will talk about in the pages that follow.

Devotion

Devotion to you craft, meaning you can't give discipline a 90 days test and hope that is enough. Discipline is required every day in every way. You will only succeed to the degree you are devoted. If your heart isn't truly in what you are doing, you need to make a change, and you need to make it now. If you neglect one day you're likely to neglect two, and the process repeats. Make devotion to your craft a priority.

Here are a few ways to implement these daily disciplines. Write down what it is you want to improve in your daily life. Then write down what you are currently doing daily that is holding you back. In doing this quick assessment you can then resolve to stop doing the things taking you away from your goals, and begin to start focusing on the things that bring you closer to their achievement. With discipline comes freedom. Remember success is a few simple disciplines that you repeat every day, and failure is the lack of discipline repeated every day. The choice is yours.

<u>Principle 6 Commitment</u>

"People who are interested in doing something will do it when it's convenient. People who are committed will do it no matter what."

– Bob Proctor

Commitment means to be in a state or quality dedicated to a cause or activity.

Problem:

Non-commitment can be a serious dream killer. You become indifferent or uncertain about the obtainment of a particular goal or area of your life. Having a lack of commitment means you like the idea of doing better but the desire isn't there. What happens if you don't stay committed to a goal? Are you likely to achieve it? Doesn't that seems like a silly question? The answer is pretty straight forward. If you don't stay committed to a goal you are most certainly not going to achieve it. Non commitment means you make a promise to yourself and then fail to follow through. Repeated daily we become content with where we are, and we decide that it's just who we are. STOP! Let's re-program that thought and find a few ways to make commitment a priority in our lives.

Solutions:

Make your destination your priority

When you make your goal or vision a priority in your life

it will strengthen your commitment naturally. There is a saying that goes something like this, "The price is easy if the promise is strong." I take that to mean that when we know what we want, and we are determined to get it, we find a way out of no way. We do whatever is required, because we see our future so vividly that it's as if it's already here. Life makes way for a committed man or woman. Make your vision or goal a priority, think about it daily and you'll find the commitment & desire you need. Are you seeing your ideal future? You should be.

Stand your ground

Most people want instant gratification and when they don't get what they are seeking, they give it up all together. Commitment is giving what is required. You want A's in school but aren't committed to studying. You want the fancy car, but you aren't committed to saving money. You want to have a great marriage but you aren't committed to coming home when the love isn't there, and staying there until you find it again. These things take commitment. LeBron James, Michael Jordan, Kobe Bryant got to where they are because they stood their ground and stayed committed to what they wanted. Through the struggles and the pain each one was committed. Easy or hard, stand your ground.

See who you could be if you were committed

Where would you be if you took your commitment to school seriously? How would your relationships be if you were fully committed to them? Where would you be if you were truly committed to your goals? Write those questions out, and answer them truthfully. You don't have to show anyone your answers. Keep them for reference when you start to lose commitment. When that happens, pull your list out and remember where you are headed. Everything needed to be an oak tree lies within the acorn. You at your full potential, that person you see, is inside of you waiting for you to commit. Are you going to? For the next week focus on implementing these practices listed above.

Only the committed reach the summit

-Jacob Akley

<u>Principle 7 Gratitude</u>

"Acknowledging the good that you already have in your life is the foundation for all abundance."

-Eckhart Tolle

Gratitude is the quality of being thankful; readiness to show appreciation for and to return kindness.

Problem:

When we lack gratitude, we are pulling away from the present moment. We take for granted the true treasures of life. If you were starving and had just fifty cents to your name, and someone decided to buy you a hot meal how would you feel in that moment? An overwhelming sense of being thankful engulfs you. You may even cry. Being ungrateful is the opposite as you find ways to be unhappy with what you have. If you cannot be happy and thankful now, you can't possibly be happy in the future. Material things truly don't matter. Life's pleasures are in the moments we are present in time. When this happens time is standing still. Maybe it's your first kiss, a long walk on a wave crashed beach with your significant other as the moon's ambience reflects in their eyes. Those moments in time at the end of time are what we remember. Not the sick watch or car we had. How can we begin to practice gratitude?

Solutions:

Anchor thoughts

Anchor thoughts are moments in time that we have experienced pure joy and bliss. Maybe it's a road trip with your family, or maybe it's fishing with your dad. Maybe it's when you picture sitting on the beach with someone you care about and watching the sun set on a peach colored Santa Monica spring night. When you think of those things your prefrontal cortex goes into high gear triggering a release of dopamine into our systems. So our brain searches out ways to get more of that experience. In doing this we can shift our thoughts and our states at any point in time simply by focusing our thoughts in moments of unease. So then, when you feel or have lower thoughts I want you to practice using whatever your anchor thoughts may be. Close your eyes and visualize that thought, feel it, emotionalize it. It will immediately change your state and how you feel. That is gratitude at work and it happens when we are present. Take time this week to write down what your anchor thoughts are, and focus on them daily.

Being thankful

When we are thankful we are grateful. Every day I wake up I am thankful I have another day to chase my dreams, another day to hug my kids, and to experience all I can. I'm thankful I am healthy and grateful to be alive. Thankful for my family, and for my friends. I am thankful I can go where I want to go, live how I want to live and do what I want to do. I want to ask you, what are you thankful for? Seriously. Make a list. In doing this we can start to see what truly matters to us. We can get distracted by everyday life so we forget what truly matters to us. Spend the week reviewing your list of things you're thankful for. Take 10 minutes with this that way you can feel and emotionalize being thankful. You will find your days have a bit more light to them.

Being present

Often times we find ourselves with little time to share with loved ones. We find that while we are with them, we aren't really with them. We might be scrolling Facebook or checking email. You see the importance of us being present isn't just for our own benefit, but for the benefit of our relationships as well. If you decided to turn the computer off, and power down your phone, your loved ones will feel a stronger sense of acknowledgment. We all want to feel we have been heard. Being present means we are giving our undivided attention. What we tend to focus on grows in our awareness. When we are present worry melts away, warmth wraps us in embrace, we find a certain calm and peace give our thoughts tranquil resolution. Being present is living life, any other thing is simply life distracted.

Principle 8 Focus

"Where focus goes energy flows."

– Tony Robbins

Focus by definition is, the state or quality of having or producing clear visual definition. And or the center of interest or activity.

Problem:

What does a lack of focus cause in your life? Do you feel like you are accomplishing what you want? A lack of focus can make even the simplest of tasks seems as prominent a 14,000-foot peak in the Rocky Mountains. When we lose focus our minds tend to wander in meaningless directions. We lose clarity of mind, and with that, our vision becomes blurred. When we aren't focused our energy is wasted. So let's figure out why are focus is off, and how looking through a new lens can shift our paradigm.

Solutions:

Your R.A.S.

At the base of our brains is an area we call the reticular activating system. This particular area is designed to filter out information that isn't relevant. Throughout the day do you say, "Hey legs, walk?" No. Your R.A.S. filters that out because it's a learned habit that's not important to the brain at that particular time. You aren't focused on walking, you're focused on getting to your destination. Take a second to look around the room and find everything you can that is the color red. Okay, now that you have done that, without looking again, tell me all of the green you saw? You can't! Why? That's because your R.A.S. was filtering out everything that wasn't red. It was searching for a specific color, and it found it. Remember, wherever focus goes energy flows. Write down what you focus on throughout the day. You'll find you're wasting valuable time and energy focused on people, places, and things that aren't relevant to your future. So then, in doing this exercise, we can get a clearer picture on what isn't serving us, and focus more on what is.

Eliminating Distraction

Distraction is a thing that prevents someone from giving full attention to something else, and causes extreme agitation of the mind or emotions. What are you allowing into your awareness? The answer to that question is going to determine where you go and who you'll become. We live in a day and age where people get distracted quicker than ever before. We are literally competing with goldfish as far as attention span is concerned. Study after study have proven the effects of over stimulation with social media, and our cell phones. It is literally being called digital dementia. We spend so much time trying to get a like or a new follower, we've become addicted to the bing and the buzz. On average, Americans check their phones 262 times per day—that's once every 5.5 minutes! According to screen time stats for Americans, the average American spends a little above 5 hours daily on their mobile phones. If you sleep 8 hours a day, you work, or have school another 8 hours of the day and then you spend 5 more hours on your cell phone. You now have now left yourself with only 3 hours of available time to focus on what actually matters to you. If you don't control your 24 hours, they will control you. You can't possibly expect to get ahead in life if you continuously practice distraction. For the next week we want you to be intentional with your time, and re-asses your 24 hours. Do you really need to spend 5 hours a day on your phone? That time is something you will never get back. Write out a schedule for each day on what you want to accomplish. Make sure you're spending your time being productive, rather than being distracted.

Breathing

"Breathing is the greatest pleasure in life." –Giovanni Papini. Breathing is the process of taking air into and expelling it from the lungs. Let's talk about breathing and how this simple exercise can be beneficial to our focus and mental health. Every day this week take one minute, close your eyes and focus on your breath. *IN* and *OUT*. As you breathe in, focus on the air filling your lungs, and say to yourself *"relax"* as you exhale. Now that you've done that, notice how you feel a sense of calm & tranquility has come over you. Whatever was bothering you has melted away and a sense of gratitude, clarity, and bliss has taken it's place. In doing this one minute exercise you will drastically change your physiology and emotional states. If practiced every day for a week, not only will your focus increase, but your overall emotional wellbeing. Remember how you breathe matters. Relax.

Principle 9 Reading

"Not all readers are leaders, but all leaders are readers."

– Harry Truman

Reading is the action or skill of reading written or
printed matter silently or aloud.

Problem:

While we live in the day and age of information, statistics
show the average American reads less than one book a year!
There are authors out there that have made millions, live
healthy lives, have achieved in the areas you want to achieve
in, wrote books on how they did it, and most people don't
read them! Without reading we neglect to open our minds to
new possibilities. We forego the blue prints to success. We
miss how to avoid the pains we are most certainly on a path
to. Reading is fundamental. A doctor became a doctor from
the knowledge he or she obtained through the course books
he or she read. A lawyer learned laws because they study and
read them day in and day out. If you don't read and study
your craft your competition will out work you.

Solutions:

Build your library

It starts with the first book. I remember when I was told
to build my library. I actually got excited. I filled it with all
of the information I wanted. I think when we build a library
tailor made to what we yearn to learn it makes it an enjoy-

able process. Every book is another step into building our future selves. Once I got the first book I was excited to get the second. Before I knew it my home library consisted of about 3,000 books, ranging from history and science to politics and law, from self-development to psychology. A person's library shows their deepest desires. If you read a book a week for 10 years that's over 500 books. Do you think if you read 500 books in ten years those books would affect every aspect of your life? You bet they would. If you don't read you're falling behind. Any house in America worth over $200,000 has a library in it. There are secrets to the abundant life written through the pages of time. You just need to open them to see.

Schedule time to read

This is the key. You can have all the books, but if you don't read them they are wasted space. I make it a priority to read a minimum of 30 minutes a day. People say they don't have time. I promise if you implement the schedule we talked about earlier in the book, you will find you most certainly have 30 minutes a day you are wasting that you could be using to learn more in your chosen field. Jim Rohn said, "You can skip a meal, but don't skip your reading." What we read pours deeply into our mental faculties, it builds our philosophies and paints the canvas of our lives. Take time to spend no less than 15 minutes a day this week reading something in your chosen field. If you did this for 5 years you would become a national expert in your chosen field. Open the book.

Vocabulary

Tony Robbins, in his book *Awaken The Giant Within,*

spoke about vocabulary in a very honest way. Here is a quote from him on said subject. "People with an impoverished vocabulary live an impoverished emotional life; people with rich vocabularies have a multihued palette of colors with which to paint their experience, not only for others but for themselves." You see in changing our vocabulary we can change in an instant how we think, how we feel, and how we live. The words we attach to our experience become our experience. If we are to change how we live and mold our destinies we have to deliberately choose the words in which we use, and we need to expand the level of words we have to choose from. In reading we have the potential to learn an infinite array of ways and words to express ourselves. People may forget what you did but they will never forget how you made them feel. Your words have the power to build, or the power to destroy. As we expand in vocabulary we expand in our ability to reach, and give. "In the beginning was the word"

–John 1:1 -Holy Bible.

Principle 10 Emotional Intelligence

"Whatever is begun in anger, ends in shame."

-Benjamin Franklin

Emotional intelligence is the ability to understand, use, and manage your own emotions in positive ways to relieve stress, communicate effectively, empathize with others, overcome challenges and defuse conflict.

Problem:

We are taught how to drive a car, tie our shoes, and ride our bikes. We know the latest number 1 song on the radio, but there is an alarming amount of human beings on this planet that haven't learned their emotions, and or the cause and effect of their emotions. Our brains aren't made to please us, or make us happy. They are this perfectly designed ever complex miracle machine. Our brains are designed to keep us alive, alert us to danger, and to pass on the gene pool. We have been gifted with consciousness, which is both a gift and a curse. We are self-aware, ever adapting, and very emotional beings. When we don't know how to deal with our emotions we suppress, and suppression creates depression.

There is a part of the brain called the limbic system. This part in particular is made up of many interconnected groups deep inside of the brain. These groups and structures are said to be the part of the brain that's responsible for behavioral and emotional responses. Particularly when it comes to our survival. It's responsible for our ability to express fear, anger, pleasure, and sadness. So then, if these emotions are created in the brain, logically we have the ability to control them, and at the very least understand them. So then how do we get clarity on our emotions?

Solutions:

Reaction

When we take time to observe our responses to others we open up the possibility to be more accepting of their needs and perspectives. Find out if you seem to pre-judge a given circumstance before you have all of the details. Look at how you interact with others. Put yourself in their shoes. Our responses determine our outcomes. When we react instead of respond we have made a conscious decision to respond out of emotion instead of intellect. In answering the questions above you will find solutions to improve how you respond to others. When you learn to respond instead of react you open your mind to learning emotion on a deeper level.

Responsibility

Take responsibility for your actions. If you hurt someone don't avoid them, apologize directly to them. Most are more willing to accept forgiveness if you make an attempt to correct your behavior. If you start to observe how your actions affect those around you prior to you taking said actions, you can see how your decisions may impact others. How will they feel, and would you want to go through that experience? In taking responsibility you can set the tone for how your desired outcome can be achieved. Remember emotional intelligence is the key to connecting with others and achieving all you can.

Awareness

Emotional intelligence begins with awareness. It is the awareness of what we do, and how we feel about what we do. It is being aware of how we make others feel. Emotional intelligence is how we value and listen to other's needs. Awareness in emotion is the ability to empathize and identify with not only yourself, but other people. If we aren't aware of what we are aware of, we become numb to the ideas and feeling of others. What thoughts are you allowing to come into your awareness? Take time this week to focus on what you are focused on, and see if you are living up to your full potential in your emotional intelligence. If you practice this you will find improvements in listening, critical thinking, decision making, self-control, and the ability to change habits. Emotional intelligence is the awareness of how we process situations in time.

<u>Principle 11 Paradigm Shift</u>

"When you change the way you look at things, the things
you look at change."

-Wayne Dyer

Paradigm definition: A framework containing the basic
assumptions, ways of thinking, and methodology that are
commonly accepted.

Problem:

The paradigm is like a program that controls our thought
patterns and behaviors, by sheer force of habit. After following a thought pattern for an extended period of time we
start to form beliefs about what's possible and what isn't. We
put up four walls and tell ourselves that's just how it is. We
limit our thinking to the boundaries of a tiny little box and
allow our potential to be confined in that pocket-sized space.

We keep going through the motions and begin to think
things like "It's not fair. Why do they always get the credit?
How come I never get recognized for my hard work? Why
am I even working so hard? They don't even care about me.
I'm just a number on a spreadsheet to them. I don't feel
appreciated. I don't feel important. I'm upset. I'm out of here.
I'm giving up. I'm not useful. I'm worthless. I look in the
mirror and can't see anybody worth saving...." Whatever
thought pattern we engage in more builds strength and
forms our philosophy. Sometimes we get locked into a

certain way of thinking so long it becomes who we are. Nobody should ever have to live this way. So understand this, there's a way out. You can change the way you think but it's not going to be easy. It's going to require work. It's going to take effort. You're going to need to decide. You're going to need to focus. Most of all you're going to need to be committed. Controlling the way you think is a life-long game. If you're not constantly pulling those mental weeds, they'll take the garden and all you plant. Here are three tactics to help you shift your paradigm to a more empowering one, unlocking your true potential.

Solutions:

Asses Your Results

Consider all areas of your life and take inventory. There are three particular areas that we want to focus on, as they impact the quality of our lives so deeply: health, wealth and happiness. Are you in good, sound physical shape? How healthy are you? How happy are you? How's your financial situation currently looking? What type of results have you been stacking up? Are they the type you could be proud of laying claim to? Or are they of the lagging, shameful, undesirable sort? See our results are a direct reflection of our level of effort, and they're always telling us, as well as others, the undeniable truth. Equipped with this knowledge we gain the ability to see if we're on track, or if we need to make any necessary adjustments. Therefore, its paramount we check-in with regularity to see how we're doing. Take time this week to start building the habit of assessing your results. To start, try focusing on the three main areas we discussed. This will make assessing all the other areas of your life easier and more enjoyable as you will have practiced the ritual of keeping track and measuring up.

Influential People

The people we surround ourselves with pour massive amounts of information into our mental facilities. Our families, our peers, our teachers, the people we follow online, the list goes on, and they all play a huge role in developing the paradigm that each of us operate from. We all know people who brighten the room when they enter, and others who brighten the room when they leave. We have those who will influence and challenge us to achieve great heights in unmarked territory, while also having other people who are a prime example of what not to do. The rate of frequency at which our minds are exposed to specific individuals is the same rate that, through osmosis, we take on their attributes, thought patterns and behaviors. Remember, we become more familiar with, and accustomed to that which we repeat. We must be conscious, and cognitively choose who we're spending most of our time with. Take time this week to start surrounding yourself with people who will challenge you, stretch your mind, and instill a belief of certainty in your heart. The method most swift to a paradigm shift is a direct change in environment. If you wish to change the way you are thinking, then change the people who you are around most.

Read Something New

Another way we can shift our paradigm is by discovering and accumulating new information. Reading new material offers us the ability to peek into another persons' point of view which otherwise, we wouldn't be subjected to. These fresh perspectives stimulate and generate connectivity in the mind, and the means which we perceive things begin to alter. Imagine you're trying to piece together a puzzle and have all, but a few pieces placed. You're able to conceptualize the image, but what you see might appear confusing, frustrating and incomplete. This is until someone else comes along notices that you've left the remaining few pieces in the box. You thank them for their insights, gather up the pieces, place them according to their respective positions and a new sense of clarity is established. Now the image is complete, bold and captivating. The mind works in the same way. Every new piece of information modifies the acuity of our perception, and we start to observe things in a way that we haven't before. Take time this week to expand your mind with new understandings and perspectives. Intentionally seek out innovative information that contrasts with your current way of thinking. With repetition, the inevitable result will be transformational and send you moving down an entirely new path.

Principle 12 Goal Setting

"The ultimate reason for setting goals is to entice you to become the person it takes to achieve them"

-Jim Rohn

A goal is defined is as the object of a person's ambition or effort; an aim or desired result.

Problem:

I once heard Zig Ziglar say, "How can a man hit a target he cannot see? Here's an even better question, how can a man hit a target he doesn't not have? Are you a wondering generality or are you a meaningful specific?" You see what he is trying to say is, where do you see your life in 10 years? How are you living, what are you driving, and who are you becoming? If we don't have life goals we don't have anything pulling us out of bed in the mornings. Without goals we have no direction and without direction we just wander never really accomplishing anything. If you repeat that behavior for 10 years where do you think you will be? You'll probably be driving a car you don't want to drive, living in a house you don't want to live in, and wearing clothes you don't want to be wearing. Having life goals, school goals, work goals and so on will direct your path through life. So the tactics below will help you not only set, but achieve more goals as you make your way to where you're going.

Solutions:

Writing your goals on paper

In writing your goals on paper you have now made them a tangible item, no longer just a vision of the mind. This tactic is pretty straight forward. Get out a notebook, and just start writing your goals. Do not hold back at all. You remember being young having those big goals and dreams, right? You still have them inside of you. Write out every goal you've ever wanted. Spend some time on this. I want you to see each goal as you write it down. How do you feel when you see it completed? As you continue to make your list of goals, go back through and number them in importance to you. Then give yourself a time frame for each goal's completion. Once you have your list spend the next week reading your goals each morning and evening, as you wake and before you sleep. You will not only create the habit of reading and visualizing your goals, but you'll find you start to achieve them as well. It feels good when we commit from paper to action.

Forward progress

A list of goals stays just a list of goals unless we take major decisive activity toward them. When we take steps toward our goals, our goals step closer to us. How could you possibly know all you can do, read, see, have, and become, if you don't actively work toward them? Progress inspires us to get curious about what we are capable of. It's in the doing that we learn. How could you know how to ride a bike, or to walk? You learned by doing it, over and over. Use that same principle as you march in the direction of your goals and dreams. Without measurable activity, what could be may never happen. You have your list of goals, and now know the importance of immediate decisive activity. This week make it a priority to not only read your goals but actively working them as well. If you do this daily, before you know it that list will be completed and you will have started life change.

Achievement

You've got to celebrate your wins. Bob Proctor said, "Your results are a physical or outward expression of the inner conditioning in your subconscious mind." When we allow ourselves to celebrate, we feel a sense of accomplishment, we stand a bit more erect, our friends and family are proud of us, and because of this all we strive to do and achieve more. Our brains release dopamine and serotonin in to our neuro pathways signaling both pleasure and gratitude. When we celebrate our wins we can also inspire others to start taking action toward their goals. It's the old saying, "If he can do it, I can do it," and it's true. If I could go from being homeless and a high school drop out to owning businesses and traveling the world, so can you. But I got here because I wrote where I wanted to go, who I wanted to be, and then I made forward progress until I reached my goals. The great part is, once you get to your goals, you strive for bigger and better ones. Not for their obtainment, but for who we have to become to get them. It's in the doing where we feel the most pleasure. Take these steps above and implement them into your daily routine and I guarantee you will achieve more.

Principle 13 Intention

"Our doubts are traitors, and make us lose the good we
oft might win by fearing to attempt"

-William Shakespeare

Intention is defined as a thing intended; an aim or plan.

Problem:

When we aren't intentional we don't keep commitments,
we make excuses, and we never attempt new things. We
never truly find out who we are capable of being because we
didn't intend it. Michael Jordan didn't fall to the top. He was
intentional with his time, intentional with his discipline,
intentional with his vision. He became the best because he
intended it. Don't get to the end of life to only find out you
never lived an intentional life. You can create the life you
want if you're intentional on how to get there. You are hear
at this place in time for a reason. Let's see how we can
become individuals of intention.

Solutions:

Frequency

The moment we relinquish our doubts and believe in our
visons we allow space for intention to flow. The true secret
to manifesting anything in this life is to intentionally change
the frequency you are operating on. Imagine if you can a cell
phone, it sends these invisible messages across the world in
an instant, and you get a ding! How does one phone send a

message to another? They are operating on the same frequency. When you are changing the radio station there is static, until you match the frequency of a station emitting a frequency through an antenna. Much is the same with success, achievement, and abundance, they are available to all of us. We just have to be intentional with the frequency we are on. If you aren't intentional with what frequency you are operating from you'll never find the station you're looking for. The Kobe Bryant's of this world, the Elon Musk's all have something in common. They are intentional with the frequency they are on. That's why they say who you are surrounded by is who you become. After some time we will start to match the frequency of the people we are around the most. Have you ever noticed when you get around people who are doing a bit more, achieving a bit more and living a bit more, and as you started to do what they were doing, you started to get what they had? You matched the frequency, and because you did you were allowed to access to the things available in that frequency. Want wealth? Tune into wealth. You want health, tune into it. You have the ability to at any time change where you're operating from. Don't like the song that's playing? Change the station. This week, be intentional to what it is you are tuning into. Are you listening to gossip, or listening to a book? Playing on Facebook, or taking notes in your given field? The choice is always yours. As you asses what you are tuning into, you can start to tune out what you don't want. Practice it daily for the next week and intention will grow.

Exercise

When we make the choice to do physical activity on a

daily basis, intention is hard at work. We have put enough value in trying to be healthy that we are intentional with daily exercise. We don't negotiate our health when we have a clear vision of who we want to be. We know who we are, where we are going, and refuse to accept anything else. So we are intentional in what we eat, we are intentional in getting adequate sleep, and in daily exercise. There are many benefits to daily exercise. When you get your body into a peak state, your mind is at its most creative state. Endorphins flood your blood stream. It fast tracks your metabolism. You are literally fueling your body and mind through exercise. In the process you teach yourself what intention does. When we are intentional we open ourselves to the possibility of what can be. Take time this week to exercise at least 30 minutes a day.

Doing it when you first wake has proven to help set the mood for your day. Remember diamonds are made from the pressure applied to them. If it was easy everyone would do it.

Alignment

I believe this particular tactic is the key to being intentional. If you don't know what you want, or where you want to go, if you don't know what your goals and priorities are, or why you get out of bed every day, then you feel like you are just going through the motions. You seem to be stuck on autopilot. Now then, when you have your goals written down, you have a clear vision on where you see yourself, and your intentions are in alignment with your actions. Your goals go from thought to reality. In aligning what you want with what you do, you become the individual who deserves their obtainment. The planter deserves to reap the crop because he planted the seed, cared for it, and nurtured it.

You have to do the same with your seeds. Plant them, nurture them, and the crop is yours to harvest. This week take time to write where you are, where you are going and where you want to be. Then ask yourself if your actions are in alignment with your visions? If you answer no, then you know there are adjustments that need to be made. Find them and make them. Maybe you have the goal but you aren't taking action. You're out of alignment. Until your blue print matches your outcomes you'll have an imbalance. You get alignment by searching for it. Seek and ye shall find, knock and it shall be opened unto you.

Principle 14 Creativity

"Creativity is intelligence having fun."

-Albert Einstein

The definition of creativity is the use of the imagination or original ideas, especially in the production of an artistic work.

Problem:

When we lack creativity life's canvas seems to have two tones, black and white. A grey scale of mundane experiences. We approach life without any enthusiasm, or optimism. We literally lose the ability to create our lives without it. Do you think Apple would still be around without the creativity to innovate new ideas? No, and neither would any other larger retailer you know. They pay very well for people to create new products and cultivate new ideas. Creativity is how the hospital is built and how a musician composes a masterpiece. They create it. When we don't cultivate and nurture our creativity we become minds of desolate emptiness wandering the deserts of hopelessness. When we unleash creativity the once black and white canvas of life bursts with a vibrant multi colored pallet just waiting to paint the masterpiece of our lives. Are you ready to unleash your creativity?

Solutions:

Do what you love

When we are doing what we truly enjoy we are allowed

to express our creativity. You know you have had a job where you came up with an idea that worked better than an old method, but management shut that idea down. So rather than continue to be creative you fell by the way side and got into line with the rest of the staff. When we can do what we truly enjoy we could not get paid a dime and still do it. What is that something for you? What could you do and not get paid for but still enjoy? Whatever you answer is where your creativity would thrive, because it would be stimulated by the environment. Nature has been using its creativity since the dawn of time. Birds get creative in the ritual dances to find a mate, and human beings have the innate capacities to create whatever they see in their minds, if we stimulate it. Take time this week to see if what you are doing is what you truly love to do. If it isn't, what steps do you need to take to start doing what you are passionate about? Write them out, and then start the process. When you are doing what you love, it isn't work. Start living your passions.

Environment

Environment is everything. Take the human body for example, this amazingly complex biological miracle of nature. Everything inside has a specific environment in which it thrives. When there is disease in any of these environments we have sickness and imbalance. A cancer patient's body has produced an environment where white blood cells cannot grow, and therefore the body cannot properly fight off viruses and illness. Much is the same with creativity. If we are constantly in an environment of anger, frustration, and lack, do you think creativity can truly flourish? No. Remember earlier in the book when we touched on who you surround yourself with is who you become? This is the same principle that dictates creativity. Environment literally shapes who we become. A kid growing up in Chicago who has never seen wealth, or never been taught the principles of wealth doesn't create an environment to get it. Instead they create what they are around, and is why many see the same fates as the ones they look up to. This is all of course no fault of their own, they haven't been taught to change environment. Some think change isn't possible for them, but we can alter life by altering our environment.

Imagination

Albert Einstein said "Imagination is more important than knowledge. For knowledge is limited, whereas imagination embraces the entire world, stimulating progress, and giving birth to evolution. It's the preview to life's coming attractions." When we have a good imagination, we are better able to demonstrate critical thinking, visualization, decision making, and understanding. Our ability to use our imagination shapes our entire existence. It influences all that we do, think about, and create. Imagination can lead to complex theories, and inventions in any profession from theater to engineering, politics, or science. Without imagination we wouldn't have space travel, or even planes for that matter. But the Wright brothers had imagined people one day flying from one place to another. Take time this week to simply imagine the most elaborate thoughts you can. How does your life look in ten years? What about your house, your job, and your family? Imagine it, then write them down. Do this daily. Remember imagination is the preview to life's coming attractions. If you never imagine how to design your life, someone else will. Your imagination is one of your greatest gifts. Don't waste it.

Principle 15 Courage

"Courage is resistance to fear, mastery of fear, not absence of fear."

-Mark Twain

Courage is defined as the mental or moral strength to venture, persevere, and withstand danger, fear, or difficulty

Problem:

Courage is a step into the unknown, the uncertain. But the uncertain is scary. We don't want to get hurt so we rationalize with ourselves to avoid the pain. This never gives us a chance to grow. Fear is the number one inhibitor of all progress, and it is simply this: a lack of knowing. It stops us right in our tracks, many times before we even get started. Whether it be fear of failure, fear of ridicule and criticism, fear of success and commitment or any other type, this lack in courage if unregulated will spill over into every other area of our lives. In the chapter on practice, we discussed how we tend to get good at the things that we repeat. If we continue to practice cowardice, we become cowardly and in time find ourselves tucking the tail and running from every undesirable situation. If we allow fear to stop us in one endeavor, we are very likely to do the same in another. There is good news!

Fear has long been described though an acronym as "False Evidence Appearing Real". Here are three tactics that will help build courage, a prerequisite in getting almost anything you want, and seeing fear for what it truly is: ignorance.

Solutions:

Confidence

Courage is a result of confidence. But where do we get it? Mostly from the people around us. We all have someone who pushes us beyond our comfort zones. Yes, it is possible to make that decision on our own, however, we are often very resistant to it. People breathe life into us by saying things like, "I believe in you" or "you've got this" or even "you'll get it next time!" When we see others meet opposition and have the fortitude to move forward, it gives us inspiration and we find the strength to believe in ourselves. Curiosity grows, and we start to entertain the ideas of "what if" unconsciously planting seeds of heroism, bravery and valor. Equipped with our new mental forces, we start to take action on our ideas. As we progress so does our confidence, boosting morale and promising a flourishing future. Take time this week to seek out individuals who provoke confidence and bring out the best in you. Additionally, when you come across a person of timidity who might be reluctant to try something for themselves, let them know you believe in them. You'll be amazed that as you inspire confidence and belief in others, you'll be inspiring the same in yourself.

The Voice Inside

We are significantly impacted by the way we communicate with ourselves. We must be aware of our own self-talk. If you tell yourself that you can, then you can. However, if you say you can't, then you likely won't even try. This is known as autosuggestion, which if utilized in the proper manner can tear down, clear out and brilliantly weave a completely new, bold and beautiful fabric of life. See we are always suggesting something to ourselves, but we don't always realize it. If we suggest it's hard to lose weight or that life's a struggle, our brain will go to work and seek out answers congruent with that suggestion. On the other hand, if we suggest that life's an exciting adventure, our brain again will find the answers. We tend to move in the direction that we face. Knowing this, we must be certain that we're constantly looking in the direction we desire, rather than that which we do not. Take time this week to practice controlling that little voice inside. Train it to affirm positivity, courage and self-reliance. Say "Every day in every way I am getting better and better." Affirm this over and over, take action, and you will start to believe it.

Forget What Others Think

This is a trap many of us get caught in. But why? Well, it's a fear of judgment, and ultimately we don't want to look like a fool. But the reality is they're probably busily worrying about the exact same thing we are. See we all get caught up in our own self talk but unfortunately, most of the time, its negatively oriented. We find ourselves tucking our heads back into our little turtle shell when we feel others are watching, and if we allow this pattern to continue, then we are actually encouraging fear, and practicing the act of not following through. If we truly desire change, we must catch ourselves in the act and break the pattern! If we can't handle these little obstacles, then we'll never develop the confidence to face the larger ones. Every goal inevitably comes with its own set of adversities and people who will judge. When you know who truly you are and what you stand for, your self-image is strong and unwavering in the sight of criticism. Take time this week to practice fighting that fear of judgement by being bold in front of others. Get an accountability partner who will call you out when they see you playing small. In time you will form the habit of feeling the fear and doing it anyway.

Principle 16 Decision making

"Wherever you see a successful business, someone once made a courageous decision."

-Peter Drucker

Decision making is the action or process of making decisions, especially important ones.

Problem:

What causes an individual to decide to change behavior? First off, let's start with what we understand a "decision" actually is and means. The current definition says "A decision is a conclusion or resolution reached after consideration." Most of us go through life fearful of making a decision that we know would be beneficial to our wellbeing, to our success, and to our relationships, because we allow fear to stop us before we ever start. Maybe someone you love, or trusted has told you that what you dream isn't possible for you, or that it's not practical. When we are young, we have all of these amazing dreams that have nothing to do with reason or logic. What did you want to be, or do? I wanted to be an astronomer, mixed martial arts fighter, I also wanted to make t-shirts. I even wanted to be a rapper. I know you just laughed out loud, but it's true. I even did small shows around the state of Michigan. Every single one of those dreams and ambitions I had were shot down by people I loved, trusted or believed in, and so I took them for their word. Those things aren't possible for me! That was a limiting belief I started to convey to myself. I allowed the opinions of others to have sovereignty over my decision making. Not doing what makes you happy because you want to make others happy will end up costing you your life. You'll spend it all trying to please others instead of living YOURS. Not making a decision is a decision, it's a decision to continue doing what you don't want to do. So how can we change our decisions?

Solutions:

Outcomes

What do I want? When we can look at what outcome we want to transpire in any given situation we can make more effective decisions. How we see a situation playing out determines our decisions, wouldn't you agree? Of course, if you expect to win a game, would you make different decisions then if you thought you were going to lose? Again we would say yes. You see, we make a decision hoping for a high probability of a particular outcome. When we don't see the outcomes we want, we make decisions to avoid it at all costs. Change the focus of your outcomes. When you can see the outcomes you would like you'll make better decisions. Take time this week to see what outcomes you want. Maybe in your relationships, at work, or at school. What do you want to achieve in those areas this week? Those are predetermined outcomes. Now make decisions that are congruent with the outcomes you want. When you know your outcomes, you become more effective in decision making. What's your outcome?

Focus

What you focus on is where your energy will go. Right now in this moment you're deciding what to focus on. When we make a decision, and then focus on the result, we train our brains to focus on outcomes which we talked about above. For us to make effective decisions we have to change our focus. What is a change? It's a decision. The only time new decisions are made is when we change what we are focusing on. For example, when you are focused on falling asleep, what typically happens? You can't fall asleep. It's only when we change our approach and let go of trying to sleep, that we actually fall asleep. Let's say someone upset you 10 years ago and you decided to focus on that thing every time you saw them. What would you start to do over time? You would sabotage your friendship or relationship feeling bitter and spiteful every time you see them. Now let's say you decided to let that thing go and focus on the good that person does for you and others. What happens? You forgive and continue to grow. Same person, different levels of focus. New decisions come from new levels of focus. Take time this week to intentionally focus on the good that happens each day. Focus on catching yourself when you are thinking negative and re-focus your thoughts to something positive. In doing this you will see and notice as you change the way you look at things, the things you look at change. If you focus on happiness you find it. When you focus on sadness you find it. Remember where focus goes energy flows.

Meaning

Let me ask you a question. When you think something is at its end, are you going to make different decisions then if it was the beginning? You bet you would. If you are newly married you are willing to do anything for your spouse, right? We do the dishes, do the cleaning, and take out the trash. 4 years later they ask you to do the dishes, and clean the bathroom. You blow up and say, "You wash the dishes, I'm not cleaning the bathroom. What am I your maid?" You make completely different decisions based on the meaning you give to the situation. When we get comfortable we find ourselves taking things for granted. We stop appreciating things our spouse does for us, and so they feel neglected, not appreciated, like they are on the back burner. In time they stop doing what they used to do for us. Why? Because of the meaning they have given to you not acknowledging them. In time you both start to resent each other, and if we don't change the meaning we are giving to what's happening we are doomed. If you treated that person at the end of the relationship like you did in the beginning, there wouldn't be an end. Too many people lose the spark, they lose the meaning behind their commitment to the growth of their relationship. What we give meaning to shapes our decisions. Take time to really think about what you are giving meaning to this week. When you get upset, ask what is giving this particular situation meaning in your life. In doing this we can change our associations in what we believe something to mean in our lives, and when we do that we make new decisions.

Principle 17 Action

"The only Impossible journey is the one you never start."

-Tony Robbins

Action by definition is the fact or process of doing something, typically to achieve an aim.

Problem:

The law of diminishing intent.

Lack of action starts to erode our self-esteem. One of the biggest problems is the urge to ease up a bit. If you don't take action, what could be, may never happen. What you could have, what you could achieve, all stay on the other side of your fears. Most never take action for the fear of how it might turn out, so they never reach for what was possible for their life. I am asking you, what would be possible for your life if you took action? What if you did take that chance, and you put plan to action? Whatever that life looks like you can have. Only if you fight against the law of diminishing intent. If you don't act on your dreams and goals, they will soon be buried under the burdens of life until soon they are fleeting like dust in the wind. The time to act is when you have a hot idea, when the feeling is strong. The man who loses 50lbs decided to take action. He ate the apple a day and walked away from the burgers. Does that make him different than others? The answer is yes! That is the difference between success and failure. Some decide to act and some decide to wander. Those that act get inspired, and the inspired change the world. Don't neglect to take action. When you have an idea act on it! You may never get that chance again.

Solutions:

Work

Nothing gets better by happenstance, it gets better by work. If you planted a garden and didn't work at pulling the weeds in the spring what would happen? The weeds would take the garden! The only way you get a beautiful garden is from the work in maintaining it. The same is true with your mind, your relationships, or your muscles let's say. For those things to grow we must work on them. Strong muscles takes the work of lifting weights, the work of eating right. Strong relationships come from the work put into to maintain them. A strong mind comes from planting the garden and making sure we keep the weeds out. We read the right stuff and stop reading the wrong stuff. We decide to think differently then we used to. Action comes in the work we put in for the things we want. Get to work.

President John F Kennedy asked Wernher Von Braun what it would take to get man to the moon in the 1960's. Mr. Von Braun Responded with a few short words. "The will to do it." George Bernard Shaw said "The people who get on in this world are the people who get up and look for the circumstances they want, and, if they can't find them, make them." People with will power find a way out of no way. They don't take *no* for an answer, or disappointments as failures. We only fail if we decide to give up. You didn't decide when you were learning how to walk the first time you fell that maybe walking wasn't for you. No, you were willing to try again, and again, as a matter of fact you willed your way to walking. You willed yourself to talking, otherwise you would be incomprehensible, and my dialect would be as strange to you and yours would be to me. Will power sent a man to the moon, and put our satellites in orbit. Will power brought Einstein to The Theory of Relativity, and gave Michael Jordan 6 championships with the Bulls. Men of reason never soar as high as the dreamers, for their feet are wary of leaving the ground. Your success is tied to your will to explore the unknown. Everyone who achieved anything willed their way to that position. This week take time to read your goals, and no matter what is standing in your way, adjust, and continue. As you do this, you will strengthen your willpower. Do it no matter.

Start the process

Jim Rohn said in his book *Leading An Inspired Life*, "All you have to do is start with the smallest discipline that corresponds to your own philosophy. Make the commitment: I will discipline myself to achieve my goals so in the years ahead I can celebrate my successes instead of giving excuses." When we start the beginning process the early success and returns make it easy to stay committed to our cause, but it starts with the first step, the decision to move forward. Steve Jobs didn't wait for the circumstances he needed, he made the Apple Macintosh in a garage. He didn't know how he was going to get to where he saw, but he understood he had to get started to get finished, and so do you. This week look at the goals you haven't started yet. Pick one and practice each day this week to take a new step in the process of completion for your goal. You get the degree, because you started the process of study. You get the allowance for the process of doing your chores. Want your goals? Start the process.

Principle 18 Opposition

"Great spirits have always encountered violent opposition
from mediocre minds."

-Albert Einstein

Opposition is defined as, resistance or dissent, expressed
in action or argument.

Problem:

Opposition is always going to be a factor in life. How we
respond is up to us. Life is going to battle harden all of us.
We are all going to lose loved ones, have an intense break-up
or worse, divorce. Maybe the news wasn't good, your health
is declining and you can't pay your bills. You are going to
encounter a lot of setbacks, and more opposition than you
think you can handle. I once heard Les Brown say, "You're
either coming out of a storm, currently in a storm or about
to be in a storm." That's life. But the major factor in our life
isn't the things that happen to us. The key is in how we
respond when opposition knocks on our door, and trust me,
he is on his way. So how can we be better prepared for
opposition when it comes?

Solutions:

Face your fears

I read a book once called *Feel the Fear and Do It Anyway* by
Susan Jeffers, PhD. The title of that book pretty much sums
up this tactic. I've heard it quoted before, "On the other side

of your fears are the best things in life." The things that scare us can stop us from ever attempting to be great, to see what is on the other side of the unknown. This life can be the most amazing experience you will ever have if you find a way to push through your fears. Jim Rohn said, "It's all risky. I tell you how risky it is. None of us are going to get out of this alive. That's risky!" When we face our fears we realize how much time we wasted being scared of ghosts. Start today to stand up to what scares you, and do it anyway. You have to feel the fear and move forward no matter. Take time this week to write what fears you have, and then next to each one, write how you can start to face that fear. Practice every day this week intentionally working on facing your fears. Remember on the other side of fear are life's true treasures.

Resilience

Our ability to bounce back from adversities and the stresses of life directly impact how we will live out our years on this planet. There are large health benefits when we can look at stress in a positive manner. They include, but are not limited to, relieving depression and overall longevity. Not being able to cope with life's traumas properly can have adverse effects on our health. High blood pressure, heart disease, and even heart attacks happen from people who cannot properly deal with the pressures of life. The key to building resilience is to feel your emotions but then release them. They are yours to feel but, not yours to hold. Like in meditation, when we allow our thoughts to come and go is when we feel the sense of calm and bliss. When life happens we can feel sadness and anger, but don't hold onto that sadness and anger. That's a heavy load to carry. Let it go so you can grow. This week take time to look at any situation and find the good in it. It's not always easy I know, but in doing this we can learn to stand back up in the face of any adversity.

Adjustments

You are going to have set back after set back, ups and downs, hots and colds. These are the seasons of life, and just like the seasons in nature they come and go. We have to be able to make adjustments for whatever we encounter. We have two choices: make adjustments, or make excuses. You can't do both. When we learn to do battle with our indifference we begin to form the habit of following through. If something happens, we don't quit. We take a look around, become resourceful and try another way. Thomas Edison showed just what adjustments can achieve. In the age of electricity Edison was working on the incandescent light bulb. He had 1,000 unsuccessful attempts before he got it. Do you think he would have perfected the bulb we still use to this day if he hadn't made adjustments, and showed resilience when opposition stepped in his way? Nope. Successful people don't quit, they find a way. This week if you find yourself giving up on something stop and catch yourself. Ask what can I do differently to get to where I'm trying to go? It's the people who fall down and get back up that are written about in the history books. Make adjustments not excuses.

Principle 19 Personal Philosophy

"Philosophy sets the course of your sail."

– Jim Rohn

Personal philosophy is a set of guiding principles that we live by. It influences everything from the words you say, to the steps you take, to the items that you will and will not purchase at the store.

Problem:

Individuals conceptualize philosophies in many ways. When you aren't operating from your own philosophies in life, you're most certainly operating from someone else's. Who's got you doing what you're doing? The person that doesn't have goals works for the person that does. You are either building your dreams or building someone else's. Without the development of your personal philosophy, you operate from a place of lack. The one who has shaped and developed their philosophies has a certain influence, charisma and aura around them. Learn the extra skills. Refined philosophy is were wealth, happiness and the good life are. Start the refinement of your personal philosophies.

Solutions:

People

Who's got you doing what you are doing? We are all influencing and being influenced. The question is, who is influencing you? Whatever is being poured into your mind, will take root and direct your philosophies. Are you waking up in the morning and getting right on your phone, or are you shaping and attacking your day? Do the people you surround yourself with hold themselves to the same standards, or are they wandering through life perplexed as to why they aren't where they want to be. Who you surround yourself with will directly affect who you become. Take time this week to asses who you surround yourself with. Write down your 8 closest friends. Are they lifting you or hindering you? There is a saying that goes like this, "Birds of a feather flock together." I take that to mean, that who you choose to be around will influence who you are. If 10 of your friends smoke, you will be the 11th. If 11 of your friends are broke, you'll be the 12th. We unconsciously take on the traits of those we choose to be around. Asses your flock.

Consumption

We are a society of consumption. We live in the day and age where information is at our fingertips 24/7, 365. Most times we are consuming content that has little to no value in helping us shape and become who we want to be. You know, you have had some deadline or task needing to be completed right, and you decide in ten minutes you're going to start. You just want to check your Facebook really quick. After an hour of scrolling through meaningless feeds, posts, and videos, you realize you hadn't finished what you had set out to do in the first place. Most decide in that moment that "Hey, I already missed my target, I'll try again tomorrow." We then go back to mindlessly scrolling on our phones. We don't realize in that moment of decision we are shaping our philosophies. As we repeat this behavior it becomes part of who we are, until one day life and the neglect have stacked up and we find ourselves pinned in a corner. Be intentional with what you are consuming. Read books on self-development. Don't like reading? Listen to the audio version. Feed your mind with intention rather than neglect. What we consume most certainly affects our philosophes and how we perceive this world. This week take at least fifteen minutes consuming something positive, whether it's a paperback book, a motivational video, or an audio book. Spend no less than fifteen minutes each day feeding your mind positivity.

Not for what we get, but for who we become.

Perception

How we view the world largely impacts what we are willing to weave into the strands of our philosophies. Albert Einstein said, "The most important decision we make is whether we believe we live in a friendly or hostile universe." See, personality broken down is *personal reality*, or our view of the world. So you see, how we perceive our reality determines how we project ourselves. Someone who always sees the negative, has no hope, and seems angered all the time projects themselves differently than someone who perceives to see the good in the world, someone who has compassion, empathy and character. How you view the world is uniquely your experience. Not one other soul on this planet will experience your thoughts, or see how you see and feel. Nobody gets to see the show that plays in your mind. Whatever show you perceive this life to be is what you will project. Ask yourself what kind of universe you have decided to live in? Peaceful or hostile? Then write out the reasons you perceive things the way you do. Ask how you can start to see things from a different vantage point than the current level of perception of the problem. Go over your answers every day this week and practice changing how you see things. Perception builds philosophy.

Principle 20 Your Why

"He who has a *why* to live for can bear almost any how."

-Friedrich Nietzsche

"Your why" by definition is a statement of purpose that describes why you do the work you do and why you live the lifestyle you do. It is your calling. It is your conviction. It is your mission statement. It is a vision of your life and work.

Problem:

Knowing your why can help you to find your true passion, and then the passion becomes a driver for you to achieve the extraordinary. Whether it be a childhood dream or a new lifestyle, your why will push you to achieve your goals. When you don't know why you are doing what you are doing, somebody else is going to run your life. You will never be your own person when you don't know why you do what you do. There is someone out there who is counting on you to keep going. They are counting on you to do your best every time in everything you do. They are counting on you to be the example. When you don't know what your why is, you lack vision and you are unsure how life is going to turn out. You're just hoping it all works out. Life is going to knock you down, and if you don't have a why, when adversity happens you'll fall apart or give up every time. Why where you born? What are you doing here? Who you are is wrapped inside of your why.

Solutions:

Who

Everyone is doing something for someone. Who are you doing your something for? For a long time I couldn't answer the question, but I kept asking. I found my why in 2017. I knew because my life exploded into change the day I decided I knew what my why was. I was put here to change lives. To teach my children to be themselves, and not settle for the status quo. I knew the moment I started the (Chase Something) mission that I was meant to do it. I have a gift in speaking. I didn't decide I could live in my gift until I figured out that I wasn't doing this for me, but I was doing it for my family, my kids, my friends, every person I come into contact with. When you know who you are doing this for, obstacles become opportunities. Take time each day this week to ask yourself who you are doing this for. Write them down in a journal. Every time you find yourself procrastinating this week pull out that list of who you are doing this for. You're who is a big part of your why.

What

Okay so we know who we are doing this for, and that's great, but what are we doing this for? What is it about what we are doing that gives us purpose? Is it for a sense of fulfilment? Or maybe you do it because of the legacy you leave for others to find their way through the darkness. Are you doing this for pleasure or to avoid pain? These are questions we have to ask ourselves. When we get clear on who and what we are doing this for our why is now in focus. Take time this week to really think about the questions above and write your answers in your journal. Take at least 10 minutes each day and go over your answers. This increases not only our feelings for our why, but our vision as well. What are you doing this for?

Internal Compass

When you know your who, and you know your what, then you find your why. It gives your life guidance. You have the map, the proper coordinates, and now you have direction. Your why is not only in focus it's been enhanced. You see clearly where you are going, what you are doing, and how you are helping others. Without the two above your compass won't point north. Take 15 mins each day this week to focus deeply on who you are and where you are going. Write your road map out. Know why you're doing what you're doing, and then spend the rest of your life pursuing it.

Principle 21 Flexibility

"A tree that is unbending, is easily broken."

– Lao Tzu

Flexibility can be defined as the ability and willingness to adjust one's thinking or behavior.

Problem:

We've all heard the old saying "Be firm with your goals, but flexible with the approach." Having this ability is critical as we will certainly run into obstacles that in order to get around, force us to employ a different way of thinking. And that requires us to have an open mind. See we cannot solve a problem with the same mindset that created it. Most people think about what could go wrong in a situation rather than thinking of what could go right. We can worry our way into paralysis and anxiety, but we cannot worry our way out of it. Worry only creates more worry, more paralyzing thoughts, and more anxiety. If we're unwilling to adjust our thought patterns, or fail to for any other reason, then our live is predestined to a rigid series of inflexible complications. We can, however, develop and hone the skill of flexibility and have with us the power to alter our thoughts at any moment. Here are three tactics to help you build the essential skillset of being flexible.

Solutions:

Our Beliefs

Have you ever had an experience when you just know you're right? After following a thought pattern for an extended period of time, we tend to latch onto it, and our mind forms a belief around it. Therefor we must be aware of our beliefs, and how they are serving us. The great hypnotist Marshall Sylver says, "Whatever you believe to be true, is true for you, and nothing else." This statement encapsulates the notion that our beliefs shape our reality. Look at each of your beliefs and ask yourself, "Is it actually true, or have I been believing it to be true for so long that it's true for me?" We can cultivate new thought patterns for ourselves and instill new empowering beliefs that will serve us through many various methodologies. One of my favorites is hypnosis. We can essentially hypnotize ourselves through repetition of feeding the subconscious mind. Take time this week to question your beliefs. Create and instill new ones by playing personal development audios while you fall asleep. With repetition, you will start to form new positive beliefs that will lead you down the path of achievement and prosperity.

Creativity

Every single one of us carry deep reservoirs of potential just waiting for us to tap into. It's limitless and therefore, so are we. Our creative capacities are bound only by the limitations we have accepted for ourselves, be they of our own accord or the opinions of others. We were born to create. The problem is most people are not actively engaging creative thinking, but rather just follow the same patterns as the previous day. If this sounds like you, then I implore you to change now and consider your infinite possibilities. If we are just doing the same things as the day before, then we never give our creative faculties a chance to develop. Our creativity will expand only to the degree to which we practice creation. Becoming more creative is simply a matter of making new connections in the brain by linking our life's experience, as well as that of others, with what we already know and applying it to the task at hand. We add a little bit of this with a little bit of that and presto, a new creation has emerged. And the more we do this, the better we get at it.

This is the same as any other law, it's inflexible. You will begin to grasp a handle on anything you continuously repeat. No exceptions! Clearly there's a learning curve to everything, but with an open mind and the right amount of fortitude all things can be achieved. Decide today that you'll commit to intentionally practicing creation by gaining new knowledge and welcoming all experiences. You never know what might possibly be that missing puzzle piece and the key to turn it all on.

A Different Vantage Point

Gaining the perspective of someone new can quite frequently be an immense help. A fresh set of eyes can often sight the incongruity with little to no effort. That is because their perspective is of the whole, and not necessarily being tuned into any specific piece. They offer us their point of view, based off their own thought patterns which have been accumulated throughout the term of their lives. This is the power of the mastermind, as we can link with people from other walks of life to ask questions and seek answers from their expertise. Another person's perspective can and will alter ours, if it's backed up with enough evidence that we are influenced to believe them. People of great influence are seldom hard to find, if the student is ready and willing to learn. With new people comes new ideas. Creativity thrives in a deliberate mastermind. The majority of obstacles will seem small and insignificant when you've got the power of the people in your corner. Take time this week to start forming your own mastermind with individuals of achievement. Surely, having advanced through their own obstacles, these people can help you bend your mind around yours.

Principle 22 Communication

"Good communication is the bridge between confusion
and clarity."

-Nat Turner

We define communication as a process by which information is exchanged between individuals through a common system of symbols, signs and/or behavior

Problem:

Communication is one of the most crucial components in any relationship. This includes the relationship with, and the way you talk to yourself! Tony Robbins says that the quality of our communication is the quality of our lives. Without good communication much of life is lost! Let's say there's something bothering you and you're not sure how to tell your significant other. What do you think the outcome will likely be? If you're unable to express how you're feeling, those emotions can quickly become quite the burden to carry around. Eventually you find yourself triggered by even the smallest thing and react irrationally. All those uncommunicated emotions come out at once. This helps nobody, except for you if you realize there's an issue and are willing to correct it. Here are three key tactics to help you develop better communication skills that will serve you in nearly every aspect of life.

Solutions:

Listen

We were born with two ears and one mouth for a reason: To listen twice as much as we speak. Unfortunately, most people aren't really listening at all, instead they are waiting for their turn to say something. This tends to build gulfs instead of bridges. See everybody wants to be heard. When engaging in conversation try to avoid interrupting. Take a note if you have to. This helps the other person feel important and understood, while also giving you a point to come back to when it's appropriate. Show an interest in them by smiling, nodding, leaning in and being attentive. Focus on their body language, their cues and the emotions in their words. This helps create a bridge of trust necessary for building meaningful relationships. Take time this week to focus on listening more that you want to be listened to. If you can divert your full attention from yourself to others you will find most of your troubles seem to melt away.

Self-Mastery

Deciding to start and commit to the process of self-mastery is of the utmost importance. Self-mastery means having total control over your thoughts, emotions and actions. Speaking to someone of this regard is always a pleasure because they know exactly who they are. This gives them a rock-solid ground to walk on. They are honest, unbiased and serene. These conversations leave an impact on us, and we remember them very well because of how they made us feel. So ask yourself today, "Who am I, and what do I do?" Start to develop a higher level of self-mastery and get to know your true self. Define your character and decide exactly how you would like to represent yourself. Don't allow the opinions of others to sway your integrity. Try to cast out all bias and take a step back to see things for what they really are, allowing their natural light to shine. This helps give us a clearer picture on life and a new perspective, permitting us the ability to stand strong like the oak and tall like the mountain in the mist of any storm and respond properly in any situation.

Know the Facts

Part of good communication is having something good to say. What if your best friend told you that one of his parents just unexpectedly passed away? If you haven't ever experienced the pain of a lost close relative, you might not know how to respond or what to say. Your best friend is seeking comfort and guidance and you might not seem too valuable in that moment. I'm not suggesting the loss of a loved one is a good thing, but it does carry with it a silver lining. People like to meet on common ground, and when you can relate to someone through your own personal experiences you gain the ability to form a much deeper connection. Your response-ability is your responsibility! Take time this week to think back when life taught you something. What happened? How did you feel? Who was there? What was the thought process that led up to the event? What were your thoughts afterwards? Get the details. Recalling our past experiences helps our memory, our focus, and gives us relevant content that keeps our conversations engaging.

Principle 23 Respect

"Knowledge will give you power, but character respect."

-Bruce Lee

Respect can be defined as a feeling of deep admiration for someone or something drawn from their abilities, qualities, or achievements.

Problem:

We've all had experiences with people who are difficult to work with. Many people fail to develop their infinite potentials, mostly due to a lack of sound communication skills. And I'm referring predominantly to people communicating with themselves. See, how you talk to yourself is how you will talk to other people. If you don't have much respect yourself, then you certainly won't have much respect for others. We run into people like this every day. And this doesn't make them bad people, just hard to be around. When we see them at events or social gatherings, we try to preserve our peace of mind by intentionally avoiding their company. We see that situation as something to endure rather than enjoy. It's not comfortable, but if you can muster up the courage to go communicate with them, you'll likely find they'll be more than happy to communicate back. This is the same for respect. Offer respect to others and they'll gladly offer it back, making for a pleasant situation, conversation and relationship built on truth. Here are three tactics to help you build better relationships with others as well as yourself.

Solutions:

The Golden Rule

"Treat other people as you would like to be treated."
-Almost Everyone. We've all heard it, probably from our parents, maybe grandparents, our teachers, peers, anybody who actually cares.. But it's one thing to hear it, and a task to actually implement. Most people are reactional. If you're upset and lash out at somebody, very many times they think you're upset with them. If we could take a moment to just step back and detach ourselves from the situation, we would see what is really happening. Communication expert, Tony Robbins describes this as a "cry for help" and it is. It's our duty as one human race, to respond not with another cry for help but with compassion and understanding. In that moment, we have a chance to listen, and they have a chance to be heard. This helps both of us. They feel as if a weight has been lifted off their shoulders because someone has identified with their situation and shown that they truly care, and we get a well-rounded picture of the situation and insights as to how we can help them. It's simple. If you want respect, you must be respectful. And that starts with checking your ego, and deliberately practicing your communication skills, with listening being at the forefront.

Self-Image

Who do you see when you look in the mirror? How do you speak to yourself? Are your thoughts building your self-esteem or beating you down? Do you see somebody worth saving? Somebody worth investing time, energy and resources into? Or do you just take it for what it is and say things like, "This is my body, these are my stars, this is all I'll ever be, I guess that's all this life has to offer me." The problem is your brain is always searching through your past experiences for the answers to validate what you are saying. Once you have this validation it starts to reinforce that belief. Nobody will ever take more from this world then they believe they are worth. If you find yourself struggling with self-confidence, surely your thoughts haven't been reinforcing a positive self-image. Stop this now! Detach yourself from who you used to be and focus on who you could become. Stop living in the past and start to cultivate a better future for yourself, as well as those around you. I know it can be hard to let go, for some things especially, but in order to advance in your life and develop a new self-image, just like the snake sheds his worn-out skin, you must shed yours. Commit to your better future and sacrifice your old way of thinking. Build yourself up with positive self-talk and reinforce it by following through with action.

Be Humble

It's hard to have complete respect for someone who is egotistical and braggadocios. They're always showing out trying to get someone's attention, constantly seeking the approval of others to validate their opinion of themselves. We understand these individuals care more about their own success and affluence than most anyone else's. A surefire way to lose someone's respect is to show them that you don't really care. Folks like this are self-centered and we should not allow them to sway our way of thinking. When we nurture a thought pattern through ego the inevitable paradigm is narcissistic and our connection with the world is all but lost. If possible, people like this should be avoided and if not completely, then we should deliberately limit our time around them. We can't allow their illusion of success to influence us, but instead see it for what it is: just an illusion. Let your results speak for you, as they will certainly speak louder than your words. Offer credit where credit is due. Nobody has ever gotten where they are by themselves. Yes, by the effort of their own willpower, but certainly they've received help from someone, even if it was a piece of information. Take inventory of the people in your life who have helped you along in your journey. Reach out to them and assert how much you appreciate everything they have done for you. This will build a more powerful relationship and multiply their respect for you tenfold.

Principle 24 Fear

"Have no fear of perfection-you'll never reach it."
-Salvador Dali

Fear is an unpleasant emotion caused by the belief that someone or something is dangerous, likely to cause pain, or a threat.

Problem:

Fear is engrained in our DNA. It's what kept the caveman alive. These responses lie within the amygdala. This particular area of the brain is the fight or flight mechanism. Fear is debilitating as it can cause inaction, the inability to move, and we put the parking brake of life on. Let's say you're in class or at a meeting and you don't understand a particular question or problem that everyone else understands, and rather than raise your hand to get help, you sit silently because you are scared of what other people will think of you for asking. There is an old acronym for fear that goes something like this. Fear stands for "False Evidence Appearing Real." This means 90% of the problems we think will happen never do. Yet we feel the pain in our minds and because we have painted this false reality we become complacent and immobilized. The good news is if you take time this week to implement the strategies we have laid out below, you can start to turn fear into courage, and immobilization into action.

Solutions:

Searching for the Unknown

See we all feel fear when we approach the unknown. We make up all these different possibilities and outcomes in our minds. "What if this doesn't work out? What if I lose it all, or what if it works out how we imagined?" You see if we don't step into the unknown we can never go forward. The unknown is on the outside of our comfort zones. Think about all of the good, and possibilities that lie beyond your comfort of the known. The only thing required for you to get those possibilities is to act. The decision to move from where we are to where we want to be. Imagine if you will playing a game of baseball. You're up to bat. The bases are loaded, it's the bottom of the 9th, you're down by 3. The team is depending on you to hit a homerun. Fear takes over. Your brain is coming up with a million ways you could fail. You could, foul, walk, or strike out. There are just two choices, back away from the fear, or step into the unknown and take a swing. You will miss 100% of the pitches you don't take a swing at. This week step into the unknown and see what you are truly capable of. Do what scares you, and you'll find that in the unknown all possibilities exist.

Get off the surface

You see most times when we come up with the reasons that hold us back, we don't take the time to actually process what's causing the fear in the first place. In analyzing our fears and digging below the surface we begin to see that the problem isn't actually a problem but rather our perception of our current circumstances. I read this great passage in a book entitled *Mindfulness for Beginners* by Jon Kabat Zinn that really ties into this, and I'd like to paraphrase it for you. Fear is like the ocean. On the ocean surface it can be wildly untamed and ferocious to the point that you couldn't discern it as a surface anymore. Yet in the midst of the most ferocious turbulence, if you would just descend beneath the surface 20-30 foot down you will find no turbulence at all, just gentle calm undulation. Our mind is much the same. Changing constantly the weather patterns of our lives, our emotions, our fears, and thoughts, often with no awareness on our part. We can mistake them for truths or reality when in actuality they are just waves on the surface. Remember if you want to break free of the turbulent storms and waves you have to get off the surface, and ask why you have those fears in the first place. This week take time to get quiet, go in your mind and get beneath the surface. Analyze what you are fearful of and you'll find most of what you fear never comes to pass. They say FEAR stands for, False Evidence Appearing Real. Fear is the surface, get below it.

Just do it

I spent many years not chasing my dreams because of my fears. I was scared to lose friends, disappoint my family, and quiet honestly sacred to fail. What I have come to learn is in doing it anyway, I broke through many of the barriers I thought where going to stop me. People would tell me my dreams weren't possible for me, and I believed them. I was scared to start a business, but I did it, and now I own 5. I was scared to travel for a long time, for the fear of what could happen in the wilderness alone. However I did it anyway and have had the most amazing experiences because of it. I was fearful of climbing mountains. I could fall, be struck by lightning, or even become lost and succumb to the elements. Did I allow it to stop me? No, I have climbed and summited twelve 14,000 foot mountains because of it. I have even summited a few with Mike. I was scared to tell my story to the world for the fear that nobody would want to hear it. It turned out my story inspired more than I ever imagined, and now Mike and I travel speaking to people, showing them what's possible if they just do it. Two years ago I couldn't imagine doing what I am doing now. However none of those things would have come to fruition had I allowed fear to stop me. Where would you be if you did the things that scared you? What would you be able to accomplish if fear wasn't a factor in your life? That decision always lies with you and only you. I suggest if you are fearful to start a business, join a team, or to speak to people, to do it anyway, as this builds confidence, and self-esteem. Feel the fear and do it anyway.

Principle 25 Taking Ownership

"When you think everything is someone's fault, you will suffer a lot. When you realize that everything springs only from yourself, you will learn both peace and joy."

-Dalai Lama

Taking ownership can be defined as being responsible or accountable for something that is within one's power, control or management.

Problem:

We have in us all two major forces that are in a constant battle to either push us forward, or pull us back; build us up, or tear us down; add strength and virility, or eat away at our soul. As one loses traction, the other one gains it. One does what's hard while the other complains about how hard it is. One discovers, owns and corrects his faults while the other relentlessly plays the blame-game. If we don't take control, then one of these forces will. And it will be the one that's been fed more. We all get to choose who we want to be and how we respond to things, feeding either the victor or the victim. Let's consider the victim: timid, shy, fearful and irresponsible. This person can never get very far in life, while operating primarily from this mentality, because he has forfeited his responsibility. In other words, his hands are off the wheel. He has surrendered all control over his destination and will always end up finding himself in undesirable situations because he never took ownership of where he's going and how he gets there. He so willingly blames circumstance and other people while unconsciously abandoning the chance to learn and grow, and then wonders, "why me?" Here are three tactics that will help you avoid the victim's mentality and take control of your life.

Solutions:

The Power of The Will

We've all heard someone say, "I have no willpower." I'm going to tell you that's B.S. We all have willpower! What they really mean is their willpower is untrained and weak after neglecting to follow through with their decisions on several different occasions. When we give ourselves a choice and elect the easier option, we are sending a signal to the subconscious mind that we're unprepared to handle the other. This promotes fear and procrastination in doing what's difficult. Practice tuning out that little voice in your head and follow your heart. That voice will tell you to do what's easy and convenient while your heart will tell you to do what's right for you. If you're on a run and approach a hill, that voice will say something like, "Pull back and conserve your energy" while the heart says, "Lean in and conquer!" If you do this, you will have proven to yourself that you are in control, planting in the mental garden seeds of decision, courage and self-reliance. By continuing to choose the more difficult path, you are training and strengthening your willpower to new levels that allow you to take on even bigger challenges.

Be Solution Oriented

Very often we as humans face adversity, and instead of

instantly moving towards the solution, we stop and stare at the problem like a deer in headlights. Unfortunately, what happens to the deer most of the time? They get knocked on their back, bruised and battered. If only the deer could've been solution oriented, he might have thought to move sooner. Fear kept him right where he was at until it was too late to act. We've all faced a situation of adversity when uncertainty obscured our judgment. In not knowing which actions to take, we do nothing for fear of making the wrong move. We obsess over the problem but everything we associate with it is negative, so our self-talk is negative. We start looking for all the reasons why it can't be done and forming beliefs about not being able to handle it. In not acting, we call upon very few mental faculties and our brain is robbed of a chance to allow its creative potential to shine. As hard as it may be, try to focus on the solution instead of the problem. Try to have a positive attitude towards it. Stop saying things like, "It can't be done!" This is a statement and shuts the mind down. Instead ask yourself a question like, "How can it be done?" This revs up your creative energy and with concentration and persistence, you will find the answer.

Motivational Videos

People of great influence all have one thing in common and that's their ability to control that little voice inside, and deliberately choose positive thinking over negative. They understand the detrimental effects of negative self-talk and intentionally avoid it. They value their mind and continually feed it positive, innovative information. This allows their creative faculties to thrive which puts them in an unstoppable position where nothing can hold them back. I'm here to tell you there's nothing holding you back but yourself. In this digital world we all have access to influential people, so there's no excuse for not having them in your corner. It has been said that if you change just 10% of your thinking, then you could radically change your life. You owe it to yourself to offer at least 10% of your time to the development of your mind. That's 2.4 hours a day. With our busy schedules and hectic lifestyles, I know it can be hard to find an extra couple hours each and every day to focus on feeding the mind. This is where motivational videos come in handy, as you can play them in the background during everyday activities. Sometimes it's best to cut off the radio and replace what might be vulgar and abusive lyrics with positive, inspirational messages. These people have taken ownership of their lives and the responsibility that comes with it. Now I ask you, "Will you let them influence you to do the same?"

Principle 26 Do all you can

"Do what you can, with what you have, where you are."
–Theodore Roosevelt

The definition of doing all you can is to make the utmost effort. To do whatever is necessary.

Problem:

This principle can be summed up with one word: effort. The strength of the effort is the measure of the result. Meaning you can't expect an extraordinary outcome without an extraordinary level of effort. They say the only difference between ordinary and extraordinary is that little extra. This comes down to your character. Are you doing all you can or are just skimming by with minimal effort? We live in a world of cause and effect, and doing less than we can surely has its effects on our psychological health. It erodes our self-image, self-confidence, and self-worth. If we stay on this track it won't be long before we find ourselves neglecting other areas of our lives and spiraling out of control. You see, neglect is a virus and if unregulated will grow, spreading itself across every area we allow it to. So why does this happen? It's because failure typically doesn't expose itself on the first day. It's subtle. Usually it's not until we look back and stack up our neglect that we can see the results of our accumulated disaster and we call it failure. Implementing these tactic below can increase your ability to exceed the expectations you set for yourself, and others.

Solutions:

Shifting our identity

In doing all we can do, we become all we could be. You see the moment you start to realize you can do a bit more than you thought, your brain begins to come up with other potentialities for your life. Things you never thought you could do start to become not only possible, but obtainable. When we see who we want to be and start living congruent with their beliefs and values, those things start to manifest into our lives. Start dressing like the future you would dress. Start acting like the future you would act. Start talking like the future you would talk. In doing this, who we were starts to fade away like a summer sunset gives way to a starlit sky. This week practice doing what the future you would do, and in doing so you'll start to shift your identity from who you are to who you could be.

Family

Can you remember when you were young and you wanted that new bike, but your dad said you had to get straight A's? What happened? You started to study like you never studied before. You showed up to school early and you stayed late. You asked questions, and you solved problems. Why? Because you understand that in giving your best and doing all you could do, the likelihood of you getting that bike became a real tangible goal, and in the process of higher achievement you made your father proud. When you got the bike it impacted how your dad viewed you. You saw in a moment that in doing all you can do your relationship with your family grew as well. If you're older and have children of your own, don't you want them to have the best life they can possibly have? Aren't you willing to do whatever it takes to feed them, to shelter them, and to nurture their minds? Most would say yes, but when it comes to ourselves we give a little less than we should. Start today to focus on who you're doing this for, even if it's yourself, because the most important person we need to be proud of is ourselves. You can't pour from an empty cup.

Reflect

Think back to a time when you felt unstoppable, as if you were on the top of the world. What were you doing in those moments that produced those feelings of elation? Most likely you were applying yourself the best ways you knew how to. You were striving for your best, and in doing so, realized that you were much more capable than imagined. A new belief was formed and your self-confidence grew to new heights. You knew you were capable of more so you did more. How do you measure up today? Is there something fueling your ambition, pushing you to perform at your best? Take time each day this week to recall different instances when you were applying yourself diligently. Consider the mindset you had then and compare it to the one you have now. In doing this you'll find that you were chasing something you wanted dearly and as a result you gave your best effort. Remember what Steve Jobs said, "You cannot connect the dots looking forward, you can only connect them looking back." Reflections teach lessons for progressions. What will you do today?

Principle 27 Leadership

"Everything rises and falls on leadership."

-John Maxwell

Leadership by definition is the capacity to have an effect on the character, development, or behavior of someone or something, or the effect itself.

Problem:

There are a few things that come to mind when we talk about common problems with poor leadership skills. They include but are not limited to, lack of responsibility (not taking ownership of problems and coming up with solutions), conflict (arguments, or disagreements), difficulty with change (things become different, or modified), communication problems (problems with conveying or sharing ideas or feelings), low morale (a lack of concern with the principles of right or wrong), a lack of enthusiasm (poor energy, emotion, and passion). I digress. Imagine a flea if you will. They are capable of jumping 200 times their own body. You place a flea in a jar and put a lid on it what happens? The flea, while more than capable of leaping out of the jar, cannot. Why? The lid. A barrier stopping it from reaching its full potential. Much is the same when we put a lid on our leadership. If you aren't willing to grow neither can your team, your family, or whoever you are leading, because remember we are all leading someone.

Solutions:

Attitude

I have heard it said that your attitude will determine your altitude. The great part about having a positive attitude is it can attract people to you. At the end of the day nobody wants to follow someone who is sad, and consequently always projecting sadness. People who are in the darkness are looking for a positive person shining their light. When you are positive it can boost morale. People are more responsive to an individual who has humility and compassion for every person they come in contact with. Your attitude is going to determine how high you soar. Choose to cultivate positivity every day this week. We become what we think about.

Adaption

A great leader doesn't make excuses, they make adjustments. When a problem arises they don't give up. They look to find a solution. When it doesn't work, they try another way. It is only when we asses a problem that a solution can be found. When we refuse to adapt and change, problems turn into conflicts, and conflicts turn into resentments. Having the ability to step back and asses your situation and make the necessary adjustments can be the difference in a great leader or a poor leader. Take time this week to make adjustments rather than excuses. If you find yourself making an excuse, acknowledge it and see how you can adjust in the moment. If you practice this every day for the week, you will notice you catch yourself more often adjusting, rather than coming up with excuses. Make the adjustments.

Communication

If you cannot communicate your ideas on what you know

or what to expect from others, you cannot become an effective leader. Good communication skills are essential to building any relationship. With good communication you are likely to have less misunderstanding and frustration. A big part of communication is *listening*. If you cannot let someone else express their feelings or ideas, you'll never truly connect with them. People want to feel like they have been heard, and understood. They want to feel like someone cares. Are you talking half as much as you listen? Think about it, like we said earlier in the book that's why you have two ears and one mouth. Listen more, talk less. This week practice listening intently to whoever you speak to. Engage with them. Nod when you agree with them. This shows you are listening. Respond when you mishear something. Example: "So what I think you meant was....." When you engage in conversation like this, you are able to connect, and when you connect your communication skills increase. Listen then speak.

Principle 28 Thinking

"All the resources we need are in the mind."

-Theodore Roosevelt

Thinking can be defined as the process of using the mind to consider or reason about something.

Problem:

Conformity. It's very often we find ourselves allowing other people to do our thinking for us. Someone thought out and planned this job and just we do it. Someone thought out and planned this curriculum and we just follow it. Someone thought out and planned our meals and we just eat them, most of the time without even considering what we're actually consuming. Why is it that we tend not to put much thought into the things we do and why we do them? Are we really doing it for the fulfillment we get from it and pride in knowing what we're doing is making a difference? Or are we doing it because it's what we did yesterday, or worse, what everyone else is doing? If you're just doing today that which you've done yesterday, then you'll do tomorrow what has been done today and the pattern will continue to repeat itself. If you're just doing what the next man does, then you are living his life and not truly yours. I'm telling you if you don't stop to think through and plan your life, then other people will, and you'll just live it. We all have deep reservoirs of potential and an unlimited capacity for learning. If we choose to, we can cultivate a creative mind and promise ourselves an aptitude that is ever expanding. Here are three tactics to help you practice thinking for yourself and laying the foundation for many years of building a glorious sky-scraper that transcends into the heavens.

Solutions:

Go Against the Grain

Mark Twain said, "Whenever you find yourself on the side of the majority, it's time to pause and reflect." In other words, if you notice you were doing what everyone else is doing, stop! Most people aren't thinking for themselves and are just following the crowd. We are not sheep. We are human beings, and we have been granted the dignity of choice. We are not migratory birds and we do not have to fly south for the winter. If you do, then do it by choice. We can choose to go north instead, or any other direction we desire for that matter. Stop following the crowd as most are taking the easy route through life. If you always do what's easy and convenient, then you never give yourself a chance to build mental strength and resilience. When facing new challenges, which we most certainly will, the essential resolve to see it through will not have been established and life will seem as if it's a struggle. Choose to do the things that they would rather not. Do it consistently and do it well. By the very nature of it you are actively moving in an uncommon direction and separating yourself from the masses. The common man tells a common story. What does your story say about you? Keep moving in the direction that feels most right for you, and don't allow anyone who isn't in alignment with your goals to influence you to do otherwise. Don't live their life, live yours.

Be Aware

Awareness is one of those blessings bestowed upon all of us yet sadly, is vastly underutilized. All too often we get caught up with life's distractions and aren't even aware of it. A bit of time goes by here and a little more there. We find ourselves just going through the motions, trying to avoid stress and get through the day. We put our head down and just try to get through the week, focused on a day or two of tension relieving activities. With all these distractions it seems like we are just going, going, going, and naturally we are looking for a break. But we can get caught up in this dangerous thought pattern. If we are influenced by the desire for instant gratification, then that is what we will pursue and practice. Earl Nightingale said that most people are influenced by their desire for pleasing activities and are constantly engaging in tension-relieving hobbies that will gratify their desires without delay. On the other hand, successful people are influenced by the desire for pleasing results, and focus on goal-achieving actions that produce their desired outcome. How aware are you to all this in your day-to-day activities? Consider what has been influencing you. What are you really after? Don't just follow the crowd. Be aware and seek clarity. We all need something that pulls us into the future; a worthy ideal that illuminates the path for its attainment. When you can focus on a desired result, all those little mundane tasks won't appear so tedious and overwhelming, but rather you understand that they are just part of the process.

Five Ideas a Day

This is where the magic happens. In forcing yourself to sit down and think about ideas that serve your life's mission, you're simultaneously strengthening your willpower, concentration and creative faculties. The good book says, "Seek and ye shall find" and if you are consistently developing and acting on potential possibilities, it's only a matter of time before you hit a home run. However, you'll need the proper equipment to play the game. See without a goal the pitcher has no ball to throw. With no tools the batter has nothing to swing. And without a plan there are no bases to follow. If you want to win in life you need to understand how the game is played. Observe what the winners do and assimilate their way of thinking and actions. Take note and avoid doing what the failures do. In gaining awareness of the two different personality types, we can see they each have a distinct set of habits and rituals. One has built the habit of producing results, and the other one has built the habit of producing excuses. One is constantly looking for ways to get after it, while the other is constantly looking for ways to get out of it. Either way we are cultivating ideas and it requires the same amount of energy. Be sure you are utilizing your time, energy and resources to the best of your ability. It's up to you.

Principle 29 Purpose

"Life is never made unbearable by circumstances, but
only by lack of meaning and purpose"

–Victor Frankl

Purpose by definition is, the reason for which something
is done or created or for which something exists.

Problem:

A lack of purpose can, and will make us feel inadequate
in every aspect of life. We almost feel numb to all emotion,
just going through the motions of each day without direction. Without purpose desire dies. You stop doing what you
said you would, and within a few weeks your dreams are
buried and forgotten. You start living a life not meant for
you, and because how you think your life should be, versus
how it is now doesn't match, you feel pain. The good news is,
you can dig the dirt off of your goals, and rekindle your
flame as you rediscover your purpose. Here are a few tactics
for you to practice this week on rediscovering your purpose.

Solutions:

What wakes you up

I don't mean your alarm, your mom, or any outside
circumstance. There is something inside you that wakes you,
it sets the sun, blooms the flower, blows the wind, and beats
your heart. So every day you are allowed another day on this
planet means your still have a purpose to fulfill. The odds of

your birth are 400 trillion to 1. Do you understand how lucky you are to be here? We all have a purpose. You were born not just to exist, but to experience all this life has to offer. Why were you put here? Who are you doing this for? Write down where you see yourself 3 years from now, and why you are doing what you're doing. Think every morning for the next week about those questions above, and write your answers down and read them too. You don't need to show anyone your answers, they are for you. In doing this, your purpose will begin to come into focus and life opens in new and amazing ways. They say when the student is ready the teacher will appear. If you ask those questions long enough you'll get below the surface and find your answers.

Purpose is calling, pick up the phone.

Stop holding limited beliefs

When we are young we have these big dreams and big goals, but somewhere along the road somebody we loved and trusted told us that what we were dreaming wasn't possible for us, and we believed them. But I ask you, what would your reality look like if you didn't listen to what people said about you? What would your life look life if you decided to give everything you've got to everything you do? Limited beliefs will bury what you were born to give to this world. I implore you to stop focusing on the noise, even if it's your momma. You need to believe in you. You don't need anybody else for you to believe what you believe, that power lies within you. Look at yourself bigger than yourself. Your limited beliefs can make you feel small. Let it go. Selflessness ignites perspective in purpose.

Be you

Most all of us become who were are, shaped by the opinions of others. We tend to act differently depending on who we are around. We spend so much time being who they want us to be, we don't know who we truly are. When you are uniquely you, people will gravitate to you. In being your authentic self, you find true peace. Your purpose in life is for you to be uniquely you, because the purpose of life is simply to live it. Lose who you are so you can become who you need.

Be you.

That's your purpose.

<u>Principle 30 Personal Development</u>

"It's not what happens in the world that determines the major part of your future. What happens, happens to us all. The key is what you do about it."

–Jim Rohn

Personal development includes activities that improve awareness and identity, develop talents and potential, build human capital and facilitate employability, enhance quality of life and contribute to the realization of dreams and aspirations.

Problem:

Earl Shoaff said, "All that you have at the moment you've attracted by the person you are."

When we neglect self-development we tend to pick up the traits and philosophies of the individuals we are around. Without intentional development progress is nonexistent. Life without progress makes us feel stagnate. We can become closed minded, and we wander through life without meaning, not knowing who we are or what we want to do. A life without meaning isn't a life worth living. Without self-development the possibility of who we can become is fleeting like a summer breeze across the ocean. We get lost in conformity being like everyone else, and doing what everyone else is doing. Education is the most important thing in your life. It's the bridge between where you are and where you could be. If you aren't developing yourself, someone else is. Can you guess what they have planned for you? Not much. Be intentional with these solutions below to help you increase your intellect and your influence.

Solutions:

Progress

Progress gives you the feelings of achievement, significance, and purpose. There is a quote by Tony Robbins that says, "Progress equals happiness," and indeed when we are achieving and growing, we feel a sense of bliss and pleasure. Let's say you wanted to get stronger and I tell you to do 20 pushups, but you can only do 10. Is 10 all you can do? No, if you waited a few minutes you can do 10 more. Soon you're going from 10 to 50! In the process you feel stronger and decide to push to do more. You can do the same in your mental capacities as well. The more you work on them and continue to develop new skills, the more you become, and the more you want to learn and do. Most all of high achievers immediately create another goal after they have gotten to the one they were after. Why? Because they understand it isn't in the accomplishment of a goal, but who we become in the process of achievement. They don't sit and wander, they find a new target to take aim at, and then become the individual who is capable of its obtainment. With deliberate development, progress breeds blissful dissatisfaction. This means we are happy where we are while in the pursuit of what we want. It's not in the doing, it's in the becoming. This week track the progress you have made on the goals you have laid out for your life. Are you finding you could be doing more? Remember not to mistake movement for progress.

You could be going, going, going but the question is, doing what?

Becoming a meaningful specific

Imagine if you can, a ship without a captain at the helm. No destination, it's just floating around the sea. What will eventually happen to that ship? It will likely sink or end up washed up on some beach. Why? It has no destination, or someone at the wheel directing the ship. Now imagine your mind if you will. If you don't have a pre-planned goal or destination the mind will wander in thoughts of destitution, aimlessly producing more of its kind. Now if you put a captain at the ship's helm and it has a preset course and coordinates, what will happen? 99 times out of 100 that ship will get to where it is going. Why, because it has a specified destination. Are you just wandering around with no clue where you are going, drifting through life without a destination in mind? In becoming a meaningful specific we find clarity on our journey and are more likely to get our ship safely to the harbor. Take time this week to get specific on what it is you want, and create a road map to get there. Remember though, plans without action are just plans. Become a meaningful specific.

The vision of the future

Jim Rohn said, "If the promise is strong, then the price will be easy to pay." Meaning if you are clear on what you want, then the cost of getting it doesn't seem so large. The opposite is also true; if you are unclear on what you want or where you're going, the road to getting there seems dark, cloudy and unsurmountable. You see the clearer the vision, the stronger it pulls! Remember, by keeping your vision in front of you at all times you are setting the course for your future. Anyone who is continuously moving forward eventually gets somewhere. You'll find in having a clear vision, you'll actually want to take on the challenges that come along with becoming the individual who would obtain it. Take time this week to build a vision board and review it every day. The more familiar you are with your vision, the more likely you are of turning it into reality. Keep putting one foot in front of the other, moving in the direction of your life's purpose and step into your greatness!

PRINCIPLE 31 SELF-ASSESSING

"Confront the dark parts of yourself, and work to banish them with illumination and forgiveness. Your willingness to wrestle with your demons will cause your angels to sing."

— August Wilson

Self-assessing is defined as evaluation of one's self or one's actions and attitudes, in particular, of one's performance at a job or learning tasks considered in relation to an objective standard.

Problem:

When we do not look back at what we have done or how we have behaved in the past, we cannot possible expect to correct an error in judgment, or behavior. We typically refuse to change, and believe anyone with any opinion on what we are doing, or how we are living as the enemy. We self-sabotage because we refuse to look at the true problem, which is ourselves. When we can start to take a look at what we have done and who we have been, can we get an idea on what to do and what not to do. So then what are a few ways to increase our self-assessing skills? Remember Jim Rohn said, "The major person you want to study is yourself."

Solutions:

Insights

When we take time to look back at things we have done, and decisions we have made, we get insights that would have went unnoticed otherwise. We see that maybe how we reacted to a situation earlier in the day was not representative of the character we want to emulate. Because we took time to assess the situation we were able to gain a better understanding for how to have a better outcome, should something like that present itself again in the future. This week when something happens that doesn't go quite like you want it to, take time to assess how the situation played out and what you could have done differently. Remember the best way to change behavior is to correct it, admit we were wrong and adjust.

Reflection

Now reflection focuses more on our personal process which when practiced can deepen the understanding of one's self, which can then lead to amazing discoveries or insights. Reflection is finding out why we act the way we act, why we emotionalize what we do, and how we treat those we come into contact with. Reflection is accepting all of our flaws and being open and honest with ourselves, putting down the walls and masks we all carry, and looking at our true authentic selves. It's in quiet moments of reflection that life gives her secrets away. This week take time to reflect on who you are and who you've been. Gaining a deeper understanding of yourself allows you to be more of yourself. Spend no less than 10 minutes a day this week reflecting, and then projecting.

Identify your strengths

In doing the above two practices we find a few dichotomies. We find our weaknesses and strengths, our lacks and where we prosper, and while the decision is ours to choose which to focus on, understanding our strengths and growing them are keys to unlocking true hidden potential. Sure we could say, "No we need to find our weaknesses and strengthen them." I say no. There is one thing we don't get back on this planet and it's our time. We never know if we get tonight, tomorrow or when our last moment will be. Don't spend your life so busy on your weaknesses that you never see what your true strengths were. In self-assessing and finding what we are good at, we can shift ourselves to new levels we had only dreamed of before. This week take time to write down what your strengths are. Maybe you're good at taking pictures, or cutting grass, maybe you like to design clothes or build cars. List them and then find out which things you truly enjoy and spend more time doing those. Remember, it's not work when you enjoy what you do.

PRINCIPLE 32 BELIEF

"Belief is the starting point of all achievement."
–Jim Rohn

Belief is defined as the trust, faith, or confidence in someone or something.

Problem:

A lack of belief in one's self can be the biggest obstacle we may ever encounter. It's not what others say about you that will determine your successes in life, but rather what YOU say about YOU. When we think we aren't enough, we begin to perpetuate these thoughts, unconsciously forming belief systems that are not congruent with the visions of our lives. When this happens we experience pain. We feel worthless, unwanted, insignificant and unable to achieve our desires. We begin to have a lack of confidence and trust in ourselves. This is also known as B.S. or what we call *belief systems*. The good news is we can at any moment begin to change what we believe is possible for ourselves.

Solutions:

Raising Your Standards

We don't get our wants, we get our musts. Changing what we demand of ourselves is the only true way to raise our standards. What we don't hate we will eventually tolerate. Think about the great leaders both men and women alike who elevated their standards and had the convictions to see them through no matter what. People like Abraham Lincoln, Harriet Tubman, or Rosa Parks all took amazing steps to raising their standards and in doing so, have etched their names in the history books. That same ability lies within you. Write down what you are no longer willing to accept in your life. Then think about all the things you want and the standards required for their obtainment. Each day this week practice doing a bit more than you normally do. If you read, raise your standard to read a bit more each day. If you are an athlete, decide to raise your standards in practice. Show up early and leave late. If you're older, and married, raise your standards in your relationship. Do more, and give more. You'll find when your wants become your musts, your beliefs become your standards, and your visions become your reality. Raise your standards.

Pleasure & Pain

Every single thing we do in this world is controlled by our need to either avoid pain or experience pleasure. What is stopping you from following through? It is a belief that you have developed over a lifetime of conditioning. At times we can't get ourselves to follow through and in turn feel overwhelmed and frustrated. The major factor here is we are trying to focus on changing a behavior rather than the BELIEF that's causing the behavior. When you build a belief that says "you can't achieve your goals" you generally won't act on them. On the contrary, when you begin to actualize and achieve your goals, you start to believe you can do more and become more. In understanding this, we can then start to make adjustments and lasting changes not only for ourselves but for the individuals we care about. "A man who suffers before it is necessary, suffers more than is necessary."

–Seneca

Mentors

Seek out individuals who believe in you more than you believe in yourself, people who can see the potential in you when you cannot. Often times we get so caught up in every-day distractions that we fail to do the little things which reinforce what we believe about ourselves. Gaining an outside perspective can give us clarity of mind and help re-focus our ambitions. Mentors help us get back on track when we fall off. A good mentor understands the importance of pushing past our comfort zones and limitations. They understand this is where the growth takes place. Take twenty minutes each day this week to seek out mentorship in the areas that you would like to grow. This could be, but not limited to books, audio programs, or social gatherings. In finding mentors, we gain leverage through a new perspective and attitude. This is an advantage over ourselves that otherwise we may not have been receptive to. The biggest shifts, however, are in our beliefs. All you achieve stems from what you believe. Consider who has you thinking what you're thinking. Who are you allowing to mentor you?

PRINCIPLE 33 HEALTH

'To keep the body in good health is a duty...otherwise we shall not be able to keep the mind strong and clear."
– Buddha

Health is the state of being free from illness or injury.

Problem:

There is a saying that goes, "Treat your body like a temple and not a wood shed." What do you interpret that to mean? You see if you don't feel well you can't possibly do well. Poor physical health leads to poor mental health. When we eat junk and processed foods we feel lethargic, but our brains have been flooded with dopamine and so we repeat the behavior. Instead of eating the apple a day, we choose a Big Mac. Where do you think you will be in 5 years with these health choices? A recent CDC study shows that close to half of the adult population of the U.S are now expected to develop diabetes during their lifetime,* and this number is likely to increase. We take our cars to the car wash, we buy the latest phones, but most of the time we do nothing for our own physical and mental wellbeing. As the time passes, which it surely will, you may wind up being who you don't want to be, wearing what you don't want to wear, and feeling how you don't want to feel. Don't end up a statistic in another one of these studies. Decide today to be intentional with your health.

Solutions:

Develop a health plan

Look at what you're consuming and drinking each day. Your body needs water as it makes up nearly 70% of who you are. Trade the doughnut for an apple, and the Big Mac for a salad. Will it be easy at first? I guess that depends on your level of commitment. For some, the willingness to sacrifice in what they consume comes easy because the promise of the future looms strong in their minds. There's just a few fundamentals in dieting. Eat more greens, fruits, veggies, and lean proteins. Eat less processed foods like chips, pops, and ice cream. I'm not saying you can't enjoy those from time to time, but understand if consumed on a daily basis they will have adverse effects on your health, vitality & longevity.

Decide to start a health plan and stick to it. Each day this week, track what you eat and drink. If you notice that you're getting off track, that's okay. Make the adjustment, and keep going. Don't beat yourself up, remember the one who has a health plan is already ahead of 90% of the population. The ones who implement are in the top 5%. Make a plan and act on it.

(*CDC source: https://www.cdc.gov/diabetes/pdfs/newsroom/ now-2-out-of-every-5-americans-expected-to-develop- type-2-diabetes-during-their-lifetime.pdf)

Rest

Studies show that getting the proper amount of sleep each night significantly increases one's ability to retain information such as vocabulary and grammar. Getting an adequate amount of rest largely affects how our bodies recover after workouts or strenuous activities. I know for certain every person reading this has spent half their night playing on their phone and before they knew it is 12am and they have to be up in 6 hours. Then they wake up groggy which sets in motion how the rest of their day will go. This week try going to sleep one hour earlier than you normally do. Make it a priority to sleep no less than 7 hours per night. Remember, if we don't keep our bodies in good health we can't possibly keep our minds strong and clear. Make rest a priority.

Staying active

What would happen if you tied your left arm to your side for 6 months? It would become unusable. Much is the same in staying active. Why is that so vitally important? Staying active creates muscle memory both physically and mentally. Your mind is a muscle just like your arms, and if you work them consistently, they get stronger. Staying active also teaches us to create new and empowering habits and beliefs about ourselves, and in doing so we push through to the next level in all aspects of our lives. This week focus on your physical activities. If you can walk around the block and you should, then do it. If you can run, run, and if you need to study, study. Just make sure you are consistently staying active in both your physical and mental health. A desire not acted on soon diminishes.

PRINCIPLE 34 ECONOMICS

"A part of all I earn in mine to keep."
–*The Richest Man In Babylon* by George S Clason
Economics by definition, is the branch of knowledge concerned with the production, consumption, and transfer of wealth.

Problem:

How many of us say we wish we had more money? Money for vacation, camping, or that amusement park. Maybe you wanted a new car, nice home, or better shoes. But instead we find more month at the end of our money. We work 40+ hours a week to pay bills and have nothing to save. We get that coffee and muffin on the way into work. We spend $20 a month on Netflix, gotta have our Netflix, Hulu, and Disney Plus. We get fast food instead of cooking. Then we have no money left, we need gas, our bank account is negative and we find ourselves in a bind. Sound familiar? Most Americans have less than $500 in their savings accounts. That isn't enough to cover an unforeseen circumstance. It isn't your fault. Most of us weren't taught how to earn, save, and make our money work for us. Below we are going to give you 3 tactics to learn how to earn, save, & invest your hard earned money. Remember a part of all you earn is yours to keep.

Solutions:

How to earn

In order to save, and invest we first have to earn. So the obvious question would be, how do I earn? We get paid for value. The more valuable our skills and services, the more people are willing to pay for them. How can you grow your value to the marketplace? What is the difference between a $40,000 man and a $4-million man? One works a little harder, gives a little more. If you do more than what you are paid for, soon you will be paid more for what you do. Why? Because you have increased your value to the marketplace.

Take time this week to focus on the areas you know you could be adding more value than you currently are. When you increase your value, you increase your earning potential.

How to save

The major key here is to pay you first. Remember above when we said a part of all you earn is yours to keep? Without this discipline wealth will flee from you. Let me ask you a question. If you have a piggy bank and each day you earn 10 coins, you spend 9 coins and save the one leftover. What will eventually happen to your piggy bank? It will over flow with coins to the point you couldn't put another one in. Why? Because each day you put in one more than you take out. For every dollar you earn save 10%, and make it no less. For the younger crowd learning this right now, if you were to apply this simple tactic in your life, you could very well be finically independent by the time you graduate college. Do not neglect to take 10% of all you earn and pay yourself first. This is the first step to building wealth. As your wealth grows, so will your capacity to give.

Investing

So we understand how to earn and save. Now, what do

we do with what's leftover? First we need to understand the difference between an asset and a liability. Simply put, an asset puts money into our pockets while a liability takes money out. We can operate from one of two philosophies: spend first and invest what's left, or invest first and spend what's left. One leads to poverty while the other leads to prosperity. The choice is ours. Which way of thinking have you been engaging in? The point here is to stress the importance of prioritizing a future gain over a present luxury. Understand that there's a difference between an educated investment and a speculative one. A wise investment is one that you know a great deal of information about. You've done your research, and you're confident of a return. The other is like flipping a coin, you get what you get. Take time this week to distinguish whether you have been accumulating assets or liabilities. Be sure to do your own research first and put your money to work for you so it has the ability to multiply. We are not CPA's and if you are seeking finical advice go to a professional.

PRINCIPLE 35 AFFIRMATIONS

"Don't look for your dreams to become true; look to become true to your dreams."

-Michael Beckwith

An affirmation is the action or process of affirming something or being affirmed.

Every day we are affirming something.

Problem:

Maybe you are in a deep depression, storms are turbulent and every day you tell yourself how bad your life is. Because you are keeping your mind affirmed on how low your life is, you're activing your R.A.S, your (reticular activating system) we talked about this earlier in the book, but now it's focused on finding all the bad. Remember seek and ye shall find? You will find and feel all the bad and so you continue to perpetuate this bare existence. What happens when we intentionally affirm to bring abundance into our life, or to affirm we are happy? Truth be told nothing if you don't act on what you are affirming. If you don't act like who you want to be, you keeping being who you are. Remember change happens by a decision. So we need to decide how to change the things we are affirming in our lives. First take time to make a list of positive affirmations. Make it no less than 20 affirmations.

Like, "I am happy. I am healthy. I am powerful. I will be successful. I am blessed and highly favored." Whatever they may be, write them down. The solutions below will help you program your brain to think differently than it has been.

Solutions:

Programming our subconscious

From the moment you wake up in the morning until the moment your head hits the pillow at night, your brain is taking in all of the sensory data around you. Discarding what's not useful and filing data that needs to be saved for later reference. Our brains are like computers. The data coming in become programs. Much like a computer, at any given time we can change the program that is being uploaded to our systems by uninstalling the bad software and uploading the good. Our subconscious mind is hard at work while we sleep, coming up with magnificent alternate realities we call dreams. When we use affirmations we can reprogram our minds to look for the good in every situation instead of the bad, producing a positive outlook on life, and not grim. Science has shown time and time again how plastic and malleable the brain is, and how with practice we can in time change how our brain operates. These concepts are a bit deeper in understanding and that's why they are placed further in the book, so you have an understanding of how to use everything you've read and implement new ways of thinking and learning to your supercomputer. Your mind is your greatest gift, and if you aren't feeding, nurturing and standing guard at what you allow in, it will run on autopilot, which leads me to our next solution.

Meditation

When we affirm we want an abundant life, we start visualizing on it. How it feels, smells and tastes. We close our eyes and go into the future. This is a state of meditation. We become so immersed in the visual stimulus we are creating in our minds that our surroundings and the noises trying to impede, seem to for a time, vanish. Science has shown meditation to reduce stress and cortisol in the body. It's shown the brain to have significant increases in awareness as the frontal lobe ignites. We become more creative. Meditation is a hard to practice with all of the distraction available to us at any given moment. But this week I want you take 10 minutes each day and focus on your breathing. The in, and the out. Close your eyes and let your thoughts come into awareness and let them pass. Do not hold onto them. Simply let them flow. You will find yourself more focused, and intentional with your days. You brain will also be operating at a different frequency as you get deeper into your meditation. As the time expires go over your list of affirmations. Your brain will start to search out ways to bring what you speak into existence. When you speak it is silent, but when you are silent it speaks.

Changing who we are

When we start to use affirmations and meditation, we begin to neurologically change the chemistry inside our brains. Our identity begins to shift. Who we were isn't who we are, and who we are isn't who we will be. We begin to see new possibilities not only in life but in ourselves. We see we are more capable then we have ever thought ourselves to be. As our identity shifts so do our beliefs. When what we believe changes, then the meaning we associate changes, and when meaning changes, decisions are made and actions are taken. A shift in who we are is taking place, a metamorphoses. When what we see, what we say, and what we do are all in alignment, doors start opening and life blossoms to all new possibilities. Affirmations can literally shift our personalities. Only if we have the discipline to apply them.

It's one thing to know, it's another to do. Take time this week as you practice your affirmations, start to focus on how the person you want to be acts, and start living congruent with that identity. We can at any time be whoever we want to be. If we will.

Closing Statements

Congratulations for making it to the end of this book! Most people do not make it past the first chapter of the books they start. Does that make you different? The Answer is yes! What a journey we have taken together over the last 35 weeks. The progress you have made and changes taking place are both exciting and inspiring. If at any time you find yourself getting off track, pull out your book and notes. Go over the area you are having conflict in. You are on a path of prosperity and abundance. Thank you for letting me be a part of your journey. Remember life's a marathon not a sprint. Keep chasing, I'll see you at the finish line.

-Jacob Akley

CEO: Akley & Benson Consulting LLC

Owner: Chase Something Clothing & Apparel

Facebook @ Jacob Akley

Instagram @ Jake_Akley

YouTube @ Chasing Jake

Jacobakley61689@gmail.com

CLOSING STATEMENTS

It's been a privilege serving you. I hope you've found this book to be worthwhile, beneficial and applicable. If you have followed the instructions and implemented the tactics laid out, then to you I would like to say congratulations. You are now on your true path and heading towards your ideal future. Without a doubt, you have experienced a chance in some area of your life. I'm proud of you and implore you to take pride in yourself for giving the effort. Change isn't necessarily difficult, consistent effort is. Change is automatic when we are steadily applying effort. Use this book as an asset and review it with regularity. If you find yourself struggling with the retention of any of these principles, simply take a bit more time with it. Instead of one week per principle, make it two or more. Go at your own pace. Take as long as you need on each one. We all learn at different rates, and there's no shame in that. It took me well over 30 years to learn that I'm the only one responsible for my thoughts, emotions and actions. This life of mine is what I have made of it, and I assert to you that yours is the same. So my final question to you is this, "Who are you becoming and what will you make of your life?"

-Michael Benson

Co-Founder of Akley & Benson Consulting LLC

Instagram @mykbnz

Facebook @mykbnz

CPSIA information can be obtained
at www.ICGtesting.com
Printed in the USA
BVHW031617290422
635341BV00003B/7